BEYOND
THE
TORN VEIL

A New Age Begins

A series of articles based on concepts from the King James
Bible (KJB), both Old and New Testaments, that take our
perceptions from the Old to the New and beyond and
showing continuity as well as a broader understanding of the
original intent than may have been previously considered

G.S. FERNANDEZ

BALBOA.PRESS
A DIVISION OF HAY HOUSE

Balboa Press books may be ordered through booksellers or by contacting:

Balboa Press
A Division of Hay House
1663 Liberty Drive
Bloomington, IN 47403
www.balboapress.com
844-682-1282

Scripture quotations marked KJV are from the Holy Bible, King James Version (Authorized Version). First published in 1611. Quoted from the KJV Classic Reference Bible, Copyright © 1983 by The Zondervan Corporation

Print information available on the last page.

ISBN: 978-1-9822-6826-8 (sc)
ISBN: 978-1-9822-6827-5 (e)

Balboa Press rev. date: 05/26/2021

To

My Children,
Ron and Debbie

You have gifted me more than words can express.

ACKNOWLEDGEMENTS

I wish to acknowledge my long-time friends Wade and Glenda Sickinger, whose friendship and support for my book continue to be a blessing for me. Glenda, I call my I.T. girl, as she has been such a help to me with the technology of my cell phone and my computer since I am not as computer savvy as I could wish to be.

The time I have spent in their beautiful home and the conversations shared with them, sometimes at odds with each other over the topic of the conversation, have helped me more than I can say to be able to see both sides of an issue, which has helped in the compiling of this book. I will be eternally grateful to them, especially for the love and friendship they continue to show me.

I also wish to extend thanks to my neighbor, Jennifer Allathqani, who shared her computer skills with me, enabling me to print out my submission requirements so that I could review them without having to keep going back to an email.

Many thanks to my long-time friend Mary Jean Campbell, who willingly listened to me read my writings to her over the many years I was writing them, without expecting to one day see them in print. She truly seemed to enjoy listening to them which encouraged me to continue with my writing. Thank you very much, dear friend, for your encouragement.

My thanks to those at Balboa Press for their patience in working with an 80-years-old female who is not tech savvy in realizing her dream of getting her work published. Special thanks to my Check-In Coordinator Via Nielsen, who I feel went above and beyond in her help to me.

Most of all, thanks to God, Our Father, *in whom we live and move and have our being*, and *with whom all things are possible*. Without You, I could never have done it.

CONTENTS

PREFACE

When I first started to write what would become my articles, I did so with the intent to show how they related back to the Bible, King James Version. I also wanted to go beyond the commonly accepted views to show that a different perspective was possible.

I spent many years learning about the things I write about, both within a church setting and without. During this time, I came to see that many of the things displayed as being in the Bible, were simply not so, or were put forth in a fashion that would cause an emotional reaction from those seeing it that didn't happen that way in the biblical account. Movies are good at doing this. They take great license with the written word.

But my work is not about calling out those who make movies or television shows, etc., more than anyone else. For I have seen that so many, if not most, really do not seem to understand what Jesus taught in his teachings. Or, if they do, they don't seem to believe it, (actions speak louder than words).

It is therefore my intent to go *beyond* the commonly accepted views and to try to get the reader to do as those *Bereans* did mentioned in the New Testament book of Acts 17: 11 who *searched the scriptures daily whether these things were so.* I also don't want you to take my word for it, either. Read the verses for yourself, thinking beyond what you may already think they are saying to see if there may be something more to them than what you previously believed.

Everything I bring to you will be for the purpose of showing that we still have not understood what Christ taught when he was on earth, for everything he did and taught was to teach the people how to live the two great commandments listed in the New Testament book of Matthew 22: 36-40 (paraphrased) *love God and neighbor as self.*

My tendency at the beginning was to be hard-hitting, but as the years have passed and I have learned more about the love that is God, and is expressed through everything, as well as the lack of understanding of my fellow souls about this love (which I also shared), I have come to desire more to help them up, to shine a light that may help one to see their own path home to God is different from what they may have previously thought. If I can succeed in this, my desire, intent, and purpose for this book will be realized.

"New Age"

This is a subject that can be controversial to some, especially those who hold a belief in *Fundamentalism*.

I recall many years ago when the term first came into use regarding books and articles that we may today term *forward thinking*, were given the label "New Age" as if it were a type of *Scarlet Letter*, or some other distinction that would be considered shameful and/or heretical. It seems anything that was not in line with the present *Christian* way of thinking and/or believing was labeled "New Age" and viewed with suspicion. This is nothing new as we find in the Bible in Acts 17:5-6 *But the Jews who believed not, moved with envy, took unto them certain lewd fellows of the baser sort, and gathered a company, and set all the city on an uproar, and assaulted the house of Jason, and sought to bring them out to the people. (6) And when they found them not, they drew Jason and certain of the brethren unto the rulers of the city, crying, These that hath turned the world upside down have come hither also.* After all, hadn't they had centuries of the old religious teachings and ways of doing things— why change now? So, you could say *these* were the true *Fundamentalists*.

TIME FOR A CHANGE

Perhaps it is time for a change, for more "turning the world upside down". Life is full of change. Life *is* movement and movement *is* change. Reading your history books will show you the constant change taking place on our planet.

Those in the business world know that if a certain product or method is not working to bring forth the desired result, then it must be changed in order to bring it about. This is often referred to as "thinking outside the box". This is a good analogy as we tend to *box* ourselves in with our outdated methods, beliefs, and ways of being.

RESISTANCE TO CHANGE

While I know people will say they want change, they rarely seem to truly seek it. Seeming instead to be content with learning the basics of something (enough to get by), and then judging themselves as to how well they are doing with it by measuring against other people who are doing the same! The Bible speaks to this in II Corinthians 10:12 *For we dare not make ourselves of the number, or compare ourselves with some that commend themselves: but they measuring themselves by themselves, and comparing themselves among themselves, are not wise.*

I had the same resistance to anything considered "New Age" when it came on the scene. I felt as any other *Christian,* that I knew about God and had it all neatly tied up and boxed as to the "how's", "why's" and "wherefores". Any real difference between all the differing sects, groups, churches, etc., were administrative only. Our problems were trying to live by or up to these same "how's", "why's", and "wherefores". It never seemed to occur to us there was another way of looking at this.

TURNING THE WORLD UPSIDE DOWN AGAIN

Then along came these people who were trying to change our perceptions about things.

I saw a cute tee shirt on a girl I worked with years ago. She was going to be graduating high school soon and her tee shirt read: *Six muntz ago I couldn't even spell gradiate; and now I are one!* While it is funny to read, it applies in a way to me and the whole "New Age" thing. However, my journey has taken considerably more than six months.

Truly, the more I learn of how we can change our life by changing the way we think, the more amazed I am. And this teaching is now coming from more and more people, though it has been around for ages.

Ages? Yes! Every time something is changing there is resistance to it. When Christ came on the scene, he faced resistance form his own kin as well as the religious and political leaders of the day. He said in the New Testament book of Matthew 13:57 *A prophet is not without honor, save in his own country, and in his own house.* And in the New Testament book of Luke 4:24 *Verily I say unto you, no prophet is accepted in his own country.*

That old hindrance holds true here: *familiarity breeds contempt, and you can't be anybody because I know you.* The people of his hometown held this view. Matthew 13:55 *Is not this the carpenter's son? Is not his mother called Mary? And his brethren James, and Joses, and Simon, and Judas?* They wondered at how he could do the things he did since they *knew* him and his family.

UNEXPECTED CHANGE

The people of Judea thought they were looking for change.

They wanted the Messiah to come who was going to restore the kingdom to Israel and give the Romans their come-uppance while he was at it. Yet, when the instrument of that change came on the scene, they resisted it to the end; because it was not the way they thought it would be or should be. It was unexpected. People continue this way of thinking to this day. They want change, but only if it will prove them "right" or give them power to rule over others as a "superior" group. Superior in wisdom, knowledge, and ability. Yet the Bible tells us in the New Testament book of I Corinthians 3:19 *For the wisdom of this world is foolishness with God. For it is written, He taketh the wise in their own craftiness.* And in I Corinthians 1: 25 *For the foolishness of God is wiser than men; and the weakness of God is stronger than men.*

Do you think the teachings of Jesus were considered "New Age" at that time even though that term was not used? What *was* used is found in the New Testament book of Acts 17:6 *...these that have turned the world upside down have come hither also.* I'd say it took some provocative teaching to *turn the world upside down!* For folks to see things completely opposite from the way they were used to seeing them. Yet everything Jesus was

3

teaching them seemed opposite from the centuries of doing things in the way they had to be done to please God and the religious leaders by the understanding at the time.

I have personally come to see things in a way I never have before and I realize I was looking at things from a certain perspective or core belief that was flawed, or rather, incomplete.

LIFE AND CHANGE GOES ON

Today we would tend to laugh at anyone who insisted the world was flat. Just as prior to July 20, 1969, many would say mankind would never set foot on the moon. (I know there are still those who think that was a sham.) Yet because we have moved forward, albeit kicking and screaming all too often, look at where we are now. Technology has advanced almost unbelievably. I'm sure Alexander Graham Bell never dreamed what would come from his invention of the telephone! Science and Religion are finding they have more in common than they previously thought, and like former enemies of war that later work together, even Science and Religion are finding they can now work together.

FLAWED CORE BELIEFS

What a strange breed is a human! We tend to kill the thing we love.

We love health, beauty, peace, abundance, kindness, etc., then destroy it in some fashion once we have it, primarily because we have labored under a false believe in *unworthiness* to have or keep these things due to our "sins", taught to us by parents, teachers, religious and political leaders, all who labor under the same flawed beliefs generation after generation!

We are all too willing to believe the negative, but we resist tooth and nail the positive because it does not fit with what we've always been taught and believed. If you think I exaggerate, look around you at the news on radio, television, telephones, the internet, and all social media. Then, when someone tries to tell us or show us a different way, we tend to discount it and label them as "New Age", so we can put them in a little niche and no longer must consider them. How about doing as the people of Berea did in the New Testament book of Acts 17:11 *These were more noble than those in Thessalonica in that they received the word with all readiness of mind, and searched the scriptures daily, whether these things were so. (12) Therefore, many of them believed.* They didn't just take someone's word for it. They searched (you might say, religiously), whether these things were so. Like Thomas, they wanted proof. Jesus told the religious leaders of his day in the New Testament book of John 5:39 *Search the scriptures; for in them ye think ye hath eternal life; and they are they that testify of me.* How easily we read right over things or see them from a negative perspective, usually due to our previous programming.

NEGATIVITY CLOSES OFF OPTIONS

I will use a personal example. In all the years I held membership in a certain church, it seems everything was viewed from a negative perspective of *Thou shalt not...* In fact, it seems to me that is the view of most professing *Christian churches.* I suppose if you're viewing it from a point of view that so much is *sinful,* you will automatically be looking for what is or could be "wrong" and needs to be set "right" (according to whatever is the definition of "right" and "wrong" of that group). This puts one in a negative mindset to begin with. My point is this very way of seeing things needs to be changed.

Referring to the example used earlier of how business people change to improve things by thinking outside the box: Churches have had centuries of doing things the way they do them, just as Israel had generations of doing things the way they had done them.

Regarding Israel: Not only were they *not* getting the results they wanted, but they were once again under the rule of a nation that worshipped many gods. Maybe it was time to think outside the box. The example I refer to is found in the New Testament book of Matthew 5:43-44 *ye have heard that it hath been said, that ye shall love your neighbor, and hate thine enemy.*

(44) But I say unto you, love your enemies, bless them that curse you, do good to them that hate you, and pray for them that despitefully use you, and persecute you. The next verse goes on to show why they should behave in this way that is so different from what they were accustomed to. (45) *That*

ye may be the children of your Father which is in heaven: for he maketh his sun to rise on the evil and the good, and sendeth rain on the just and the unjust.

If you think about enemies. Aren't they basically someone who thinks differently from us about something (anything)? And once the difference is reconciled the enmity need no longer exist. Isn't this where fighting comes about, even among family members? Isn't the whole world just one big extended family? Christ told his disciples in the New Testament book of John 10:16 *And other sheep I have, not of this fold: them also I must bring, and they shall hear my voice; and there shall be one fold and one shepherd.* And in the New Testament book of Luke 10: 30-37 has come to be known as the Parable of The Good Samaritan. It shows that *everyone* is our neighbor whom we are to love as ourselves.

Another example is found in the New Testament book of Matthew 5:27-28 *ye have heard that it was said by them of old time, Thou shalt not commit adultery, (28) but I say unto you, that whosoever looketh on a woman to lust after her hath committed adultery already with her in his heart.*

We have had the tendency to say that Jesus was showing the depth of the sin that would make them unworthy of God's kingdom by telling them not to even think about it. How do you stop a thought?

NEW AGE THOUGHT

In this 21st century, where we have pretty much learned that *everything is thought first*, I now feel Jesus was giving us the solution to the problem as well as the equation for how to *use our thoughts to change our life*. He says whoever looks on a woman to lust after her... So, first the man looks. But looking is not the problem. We look at things all the time without lusting after them or incurring *sin*. The problem *begins* when we start *thinking* while we are looking.

Again, thinking is not the problem. We think all the time. It is *what we are thinking while we are looking* that brings the problem. For when you add the motivating energy to the thought (lust), which is done in the heart, you can consider the act accomplished. For if it continues unabated, it will seek to bring forth the literal action!

I am not so naïve as to think there will not be those who disagree with this writing. There is always resistance. Those who are into *bodybuilding* will tell you that it is the resistance to the weights that builds the muscle.

LAST, BUT NOT LEAST

I say to those who are willing to investigate it as did the people of Berea mentioned in the New Testament book of Acts 17, go for it! And should you find things going much better for you as you take control of your thoughts and emotions and start directing your life; don't make the same mistake so many have made in the past of then discounting the old teachings you are changing from. They served a purpose. You cannot change without seeing a need for it and that would not have happened had you not experienced what you did from your former way of thinking and believing.

So, be kind to those who have not yet reached the understanding you have, and take comfort in the knowledge that, they, too, will one day come to the place of understanding you have reached. For it is written in the New Testament book of Hebrews 8:11 *And they shall not teach every man his neighbor, and every man his brother, saying, Know the Lord: for all shall know me from the least to the greatest.*

Considering this, every age will be a "New Age".

CORE BELIEFS

A core belief is a hypothesis or dot in the center of a matrix around which other thoughts, ideas, and beliefs collect which agree with the core belief and adding layers like the rings inside a tree. The rings are separate, but some may be so close together as to appear to be one single wide ring or to overlap. Their likeness is what draws them. The Law of Attraction states: *That which is like unto itself is drawn.*

While they are not all the same—hence, the separation and/or width of the layers or rings, they all have basic agreement with the core, or they would not be drawn. For those who would like a scripture to back this up, I give you this: Old Testament book of Proverbs 23: 7 *For as he thinketh in his heart, so is he.* Whatever one thinks in his heart *is* his core belief. Many have other beliefs along with the core belief, but these are as branches on a tree, shooting off in different directions which allow the *newly added belief* expression and validity.

Sometimes from these branches come still more branches, until what we see when we look at the tree are so many branches going in so many directions that we tend to forget they all come from one *core* or *trunk* of the tree.

Such are the beliefs we hold that make us who and what we are in this present *Now* we are experiencing. Many of the beliefs we hold we are not even consciously aware that we hold as they have been with us for so long, like the branches of the tree mentioned above.

THOUGHTS TAKE FORM

For those who may wonder how this can be, I remind you that you cannot see the forces of magnetism, electricity, air, gravity, etc., only the result of them. It is the same with thoughts, and their magnetic ability to draw to themselves other thoughts of like nature. You do not *see* the thought, only the effect of it.

Sometimes we use the expression, *I see what you mean or what you are thinking*, when what we really see is the expression on their face or in their body movement, which is a manifestation of what they are thinking.

By the repeated manifestation of the effects of certain thoughts, we can come to understand whether the thought (s) that lead to such a manifestation, are even worth our time to think about, or—perhaps, we should think about changing it in order to manifest a different result. This idea has been put forth many times before in a variety of ways. Below are a few of them:

> *Change your thoughts and change your life*
> *You are what you think about all day long*
> *You get what you focus on*
> *You create your own reality*

These are just some of the saying that you have probably heard in your lifetime.

MORE THAN MEETS THE EYE

Trees are more than just roots, trunks, and branches. They have leaves, or fronds, and depending on the type of tree, fruit or flowers, and even nuts. They have different kinds of bark or outer covering. Even so with our beliefs. They are expressed in many ways; some pleasing, and some, not. Some fruit is sweet, and some is bitter. But it is all *fruit*, produced by the tree from its core seed, or in our case, *belief.* New Testament book of Matthew 12:33 *Either make the tree good, and his fruit good; or else make the tree corrupt, and his fruit corrupt: for the tree is known by his fruit.* And in Matthew 7: 20 *Wherefore by their fruits ye shall know them.*

From what I have said so far, I'm sure you get the idea that I think we should consider what kind of fruit is coming from our tree (core beliefs). Is the fruit of our tree pleasant, nourishing, helpful to and for us—or not?

Let's use an example from the New Testament found in Mark 11: 11-24, in which Jesus curses the fig tree. Even his disciples thought he cursed the fig tree because he was hungry and there were no figs on the tree to alleviate his hunger.

As you continue reading this chapter, you find Jesus and his disciples coming into the temple where he overthrew the tables of the moneychangers, and the seats of them that sold doves, and drove them from the temple. Mark 11: 17 And he *taught, saying unto them, Is it not written, My house shall be called of all nations the house of prayer? but ye have made it a den of thieves.* This is referring to the scripture found in the Old Testament book of Isiah 56:7 *For mine house shall be called a house of prayer for all people.* All people. This is an important distinction, as at that time the Jewish people who were called Israel but were only part of all the tribes that made up the nation of Israel, thought it was for them only. They considered the other people and nations to be unclean, and therefore, unworthy to have any part in the temple services or promises of God. (A false belief.)

I realize you may think I here digress from the cursing of the fig tree, but I assure you—I have not.

Now we skip to the next morning found in the New Testament book of Matthew 21: 18-21 *Now in the morning as he returned into the city, he hungered. (19) And when he saw a fig tree in the way, he came to it, and found nothing thereon, but leaves only, and said unto it, Let no fruit grow on thee henceforth and forever. And presently the fig tree withered away. (20) And when the disciples saw it, they marvelled, saying, How soon is the fig tree withered away! (21) Jesus answered and said unto them, Verily I say unto you, If ye have faith, and doubt not, ye shall not only do this which is done to the fig tree, but also if ye shall say unto this mountain, Be thou removed, and be thou cast into the sea; it shall be done.*

He continues to tell them in vs 22 paraphrased: anything they ask for in prayer *believing*, they shall have it.

Note: in verses 25-26, Jesus tells them *if* when they stand praying (the custom of the time), they have ought against any, they should first forgive so that their Father in heaven would forgive them their trespasses (intruding where it is not lawful)—otherwise, if they did not forgive, they would not be forgiven. This is from what is called *The Lord's Prayer* found in the New Testament book of Matthew 6: 12-15.

RETURN TO THE TREE AND BELIEFS

Trees, especially those that produce fruit, like the fig tree, will produce leaves prior to the fruit manifesting—a sort of promise of things to come; like the rainbow being a promise sign in the sky that God will never again destroy the earth by means of a flood.

When Jesus came expecting to find fruit on the fig tree and finding none, then cursed the tree, he was letting his disciples know that there is a *timing* at work for everything to produce. Since it was not producing the *good* fruit expected, and in that light was deceiving man by its many leaves—Jesus showed there was no need for it to continue as it was *fruitless*. It did not serve man, nourish man, help man.

The same was true of those in the temple, both scribes, priests, and laymen. They bore many leaves (*outward show of fruit*), while in fact, no actual, beneficial, nourishing fruit, was being produced. The time was coming when they too would be removed, so that people would not continue to be fed this *fruitless fruit*.

POWER IN BELIEF

In telling his disciples about the ability to move mountains in and by faith in God, Jesus was showing them the power of *belief*. Recall the beginning of this writing and the magnetic qualities of thoughts (beliefs) to draw more of their kind?

This applies to both "good" thoughts (beliefs), or "bad" thoughts (beliefs). Or better put, those that serve beneficially and those that do not.

Jesus also showed that by forgiving others they could be forgiven. This indicates to me that if there is someone you need to forgive and/or something *you* need to be forgiven of you will not have the faith (belief) that will power the actions to get the results he mentioned. The *Golden Rule* Found in the New Testament book of Matthew 7:12 *Therefore all things whatsoever ye would that men should do to you, do ye even so to them; for this is the law and the prophets.* The fulfilling of the law and the prophets' teachings.

An example of this is found in the New Testament book of Matthew 17: 14-16 *And when they were come to the multitude, there came to him a certain man, kneeling down to him, and saying, (15) Lord, have mercy on my son: for he is lunatick, and sore vexed: for ofttimes he falleth into the fire, and oft into the water. (16) And I brought him to thy disciples, and they could not cure him.* After Jesus rebuked the demon and cast him out (18), the disciples asked him why they had not been able to do it as he had given them power to do so. (19) Jesus' answer is very enlightening. (20) *And Jesus said unto them, Because of your unbelief:* The rest of the verse goes on to tell them about the power of faith (belief). Evidently, faith (belief) is something that grows with use as they had already had the experience of casting out some devils. Yet, just as some have a stronger belief than others (Jesus)—some demons were stronger than others too, requiring stronger belief (faith) to cast them out.

What does this have to do with forgiveness? If they thought (held onto the belief), all they had to do was ask forgiveness for themselves while still maintaining an unforgiving attitude toward another (anyone), they were holding a false belief. Such a belief would not only not serve them beneficially, but would *hurt* them, as they would continue doing the same things they had been doing and getting the same negative results. New Testament book of Matthew 7: 16-20 *ye shall know them by their fruits. Do men gather grapes of thorns, or figs of thistles? Even so, every good tree bringeth forth good fruit; but a corrupt tree bringeth forth evil fruit. Every tree that bringeth forth not good fruit is hewn down and cast into the fire. Wherefore by their fruits ye shall know them.*

EXAMINE THE FRUIT YOU ARE PRODUCING

What better way for us to learn that we need to examine our thoughts and the fruit of them in order to know which should be kept and tended and which should be hewn down and burned up—which serve us beneficially and which do not?

Are we living happy, joyful, productive, and fulfilling lives? Do we feel successful in our endeavors? Or do we feel unworthy of being happy, successful, joyful and abundant? Do we feel we need to be punished for one thing or another? Look closely at these for they are both positive and negative fruits of our beliefs.

If we examine our lives and thoughts honestly, we will know if there are those we need to *curse* as Jesus did the fig tree, eliminating any possibility of anyone else partaking of this *fruitless fruit*—at least through our lives and examples.

BEWARE THE PITFALL OF JUDGING

As you begin to truly examine your own life and thoughts, and to *see* the "fruit" of them, you will find it easier to see the "fruit" being borne by other people and to judge it as being "good" or "bad". Now is the time to recall the words regarding judgment found in the New Testament book of Matthew 7: 1-5 *Judge not (condemn), that ye be not judged, (2) for with what judgment ye judge ye shall be judged (condemned): and with what measure ye meet it shall be measured to you again. (3) And why beholdest thou the mote that is in thy brother's eye, but considerest not the beam that is in thine own eye? (4) Or how wilt thou say to thy brother, Let me pull out the mote out of thine eye; and behold, a beam is in thine own eye? (5) Thou hypocrite, first cast the beam out of thine eye; and then thou shalt see clearly to cast out the mote out of thy brother's eye.*

Note: By the time you get the beam out of your own eye, your brother may no longer have the mote in his—or you may no longer see what you thought of as a mote in his eye.

Let the fruit you bring forth be that which serves you and others that you may joyfully be *known by your fruit.*

MAKING AMENDS

I want to speak on the concept of *Making Amends*. I'm sure some reading these words will immediately have their guard up because they will also immediately think of something, they feel they haven't yet made amends for, and no one likes to feel guilt. It is not a pleasant feeling. Erma Bombeck called guilt, *"The gift that keeps on giving."*

In writing this, my mind goes back to the *Law of Offerings* system God gave to the Israelites in the Old Testament book of Leviticus in the Bible. The different offerings listed covered all the levels of understanding at which a person could be. *This*, by itself, shows not all would be at the same level of understanding, yet all would be accepted if they offered sincerely in whatever level of understanding they were at the time of the offering. Once they made their offering and it was accepted, *their sins were covered*.

In the Old Testament book of Genesis 4: 3-5, we find that Cain's offering was not acceptable to the Lord, while his brother Abel's was What was the difference here? Was God playing favorites? The Bible only records that Cain brought of the fruit of the ground an offering. However, his brother Abel brought of the *firstlings* of his flocks and the fat (best) thereof. Abel brought his first and best to honor God while Cain did not. Therefore, his offering *did not find favor in the eyes of God*. It was not sincere.

Cain offered less than his best, and anything you offer that is less than your best (this is where the guilt comes in), is not acceptable. *You will know!* Just as Cain did. If you are aware that what you are offering at any time is not the best you can offer, *you will know because you will feel the discomfort which has come to be termed guilt.* The Bible states in the Old Testament book of Proverbs 23:7 that, *as a man thinketh in his heart so is he.* We condemn ourselves by our own thoughts of guilt when we know we have not offered our best. God did not condemn Cain; he simply did not accept his offering. Because he knew Cain could do better.

12-STEP PROGRAMS AND OTHERS

12 Step programs and others of that genre all incorporate *making amends* as part of their teaching. I wish to submit here a different approach.

I am coming to understand that everything serves a purpose. You cannot go back and change the past; you can only learn from it and do things differently from this point on. Doing this is helping me to better understand and appreciate *forgiveness.* And the forgiveness I speak of here is that of forgiving yourself—not of getting it from others.

We have been so programmed to seek forgiveness, mostly from others who we feel (or know), we have wronged in some way. Or we want them to seek forgiveness from us because of some real or perceived wrong they have done to us.

What I wish to bring out is this: in our feeling that we have wronged another in some way is our *awareness* that we have in some situation offered less than our best. Perhaps the same is true when others feel we should ask forgiveness from them. They may be subconsciously aware that we can or could do better and their wanting us to request forgiveness from them is a means of alleviating the matter. However, I realize that most people want you to ask them for forgiveness because they want it acknowledged that they were "right", and you were "wrong".

In the New Testament book of Romans 13:8 we are told to *owe no man anything but to love one another.* What we owe one another is love. This is succinctly stated in the *Golden Rule* found in Matthew 7:12 (New Testament). In Matthew 6:12, what is called *The Lord's Prayer,* we ask that we be forgiven our trespasses *as we forgive those who trespass against us.* As we forgive others—not as they forgive us! Can we see the difference? The point being we are all responsible for our own thoughts, words and actions. As one old saying put it: *The buck stops here!*

A NEW WAY OF SEEING THIS

To my mind and understanding, when we continue to labor under the idea that we need to try in some way to *make amends* to someone who thinks we have wronged them, or we think we have wronged them in some way, is to continue to live under a cloud of guilt when it is not necessary or even helpful to do so. In the Old Testament book of Psalms 51, we find King David's prayer for forgiveness after his adultery with Bathsheba and the subsequent death of her husband caused at David's command.

In this prayer we find David telling God, *against you only have I sinned.* Leviticus 4:2, *if a soul shall sin through ignorance...*In the Bible there is a 1 by the word *sin*, and the marginal reference is *miss the mark*.

Most people would think David was wrong in this and that he had sinned against Uriah the Hittite, who was Bathsheba's husband as well as one of David's *mighty men*. Uriah was dead. How could David possibly make amends to him. David's prayer to God was his recognition that God represented his highest good—his best. Hence his saying *against you only have I sinned* (or missed the mark). He missed the mark he aimed for which was his highest best represented by that we call God.

WHAT CAN BE DONE

When you realize you have offered less than your best, *you* are the one who needs to ask forgiveness, and *you* are the one who needs to give it—to yourself. So long as you think you must have it from an outside source, you will never be happy or at peace, because another cannot restore you to your best. Only *you* can. Because another does not know *your* best, only *theirs*. Your awareness that you have not offered your best is your indication that you <u>know</u> you can do better, and you can use this guide to go forward and offer from that point on.

It is such a waste of time and energy, not to mention self-destructive, to keep beating up on ourselves for some real or perceived wrong. And those who think this is the way God wants it are not only mistaken, but are in a sense, falsely accusing God of being unforgiving when it plainly shows that when a person brought forth their offering in sincerity, *it was accepted.*

In Matthew 7:12, known as *The Golden Rule*, we read, *Therefore all things whatsoever ye would that men should do to you, do ye even so to them: for this is the law and the prophets.* (This is the *fulfilling* of the law and the prophets (prophecy). We are told to do this whether others do it or not. In other words, we cannot predicate what we do on what others do or don't do. This includes forgiveness. Do you see where I am going with this?

If we continue under the flawed belief that we must have forgiveness of someone else or we'll still carry that burden of guilt, or we feel we cannot move forward until someone asks our forgiveness for some real or perceived wrong done to us, we will never truly be able to move forward in our life because we will still be giving away our power to another who is just as flawed in their belief as we are. The Bible speaks of this too. In the New Testament book of Luke 6:39...*can the blind lead the blind? Shall they not both fall into the ditch?*

GUILT VS ABUNDANT LIFE

Sometimes those we feel we need forgiveness from are already deceased. Sometimes they still live but *refuse* to forgive. Sometimes *we refuse* to forgive, or we are unable to let them know we forgive because they are deceased, or we don't know where they are. Then what? Do we spend the rest of our lives in guilt and misery? In the New Testament book of John 10:10, Jesus said, *I am come that they may have life and that they might have it more abundantly.* You can't have an abundant life living under a cloud of guilt.

There is also the consideration that others who we perceive as having done something that requires our forgiveness may be in ignorance of it. Christ showed this when from the cross he asked the Father to *forgive them for they know not what they do.* New Testament book of Luke 23: 34. They did not consider they were doing anything that would cause them to feel guilt. Quite the opposite. They thought they were doing God a service by getting rid of a heretic.

The New Testament also shows that where no knowledge is (of wrongdoing or lawbreaking), neither is any penalty imputed. Romans 4:15. This does not in any way negate the law, for once a person becomes *aware* that he or she has caused a problem or harm to another because of their words or actions, they are <u>then</u> under the penalty of the law. However, getting back to the *Golden Rule,* once they realize they have not offered their best they then have the responsibility of *changing from that point on.* (They can't go back and undo it.) They are not under the death penalty as in the Old Testament because of the grace of God brought through Christ. (Otherwise, there would eventually be no one left who didn't deserve the death penalty.)

A SPIRITUAL PRINCIPLE

The whole purpose of the physical law was to try to teach a spiritual principal in a manner the people could understand. If they got physical or mental pain from doing what they were told not to do, then, hopefully, they would avoid that which caused the pain. Spiritually we are to come to *choose* for ourselves that way as part of fulfilling *The Golden Rule and loving our neighbor as ourselves.* New Testament book of Matthew 22: 36-40.

This realization and the change it brought forth is the repentance spoken of by the Apostle Paul in the New Testament book of II Corinthians 7: 11 wherein they *brought forth fruit worthy of repentance.* Their change of actions showed their change of belief. They did not wait for someone else to tell them what to do or how to do it. They were able to make the connection between what you think, say, and do, and the outcome that proceeds from it as well as the consequences.

We are told in the New Testament book of I Corinthians 11:31 *for if we would judge ourselves, we would have no need of being judged.* That's powerful stuff and puts the onus on us to be and show forth the best and highest in us. It is *our* responsibility, *not* someone else's.

IN CONCLUSION

In saying all this, am I telling you not to take any action physically at all to alleviate a problem you may have caused someone else? Not at all. I only want you to realize and understand that the burden of change is *yours* and that *you* have the power as well as the responsibility to make any changes that will enable you to display to the world *your highest and best of the*

God within. It is not a power anyone else has over you because God is no respecter of persons. New Testament book of Acts 10: 34.

Hopefully, once we see this in a better light, we will all be more alert and aware of our thoughts, words, and deeds; thereby eliminating any future need to *make amends.*

COMPARISONS

I recently watched an episode of the old TV series *All in the Family*. The music that precedes the show has Archie and his wife Edith singing about "*Those were the days.*" It's all about how things used to be and shows their belief that it is how it still should be.

SECOND LOOK

I started thinking about that. Each generation tends to look back nostalgically on "*The good old days*". It never seems to occur to them that the reason they are considered "*The good old days*", is because they are gone! Focusing on those days past means focusing on what they considered "good" and ignoring everything else that isn't/wasn't so "good" for other people. Things that needed to be changed for things to be (come) more equal or fair for those who did not see them as "the good old days".

For instance: They sing about *Didn't have no welfare state. Everybody pulled his weight.* Sounds good, doesn't it? And to a point it is. But the fact remains that there were those who needed the help of the welfare system because not all were enjoying the same benefits as they did as they sang their song about "the good old days". Not everyone had their own home or car (Gee, *the old La Salle ran great!*) or were even permitted opportunity to get them.

PREJUDICE AND BIGOTRY

Prejudice and bigotry ran rampant in "those good old days". That Archie was bigoted was evident to all throughout the show. In fact, it was used as the background for humor. Archie Bunker, the loveable bigot. And yes, he did have his loveable side. But bigotry and prejudice are not funny in reality...especially to those on the receiving end of it.

Another part of the song says: *And you knew who you were then; girls were girls and men were men.* This is a direct reference to those who today are termed as *"gay; cross-gender; or trans-gender, or homosexual"*, (all of whom were considered perverts), and were denied the same benefits permitted those considered *"straight"*. They were not the majority and were not even considered worthy of life in some cases.

Another part of the song says: *Guys like us, we had it made...those were the days!* Guys like us, those who were the majority rule at the time. They saw no need to change the status quo. Who cared if there were some who didn't even have the necessities? I've got mine. Let someone else think about that.

CAVEAT

Now I am not writing to condemn the TV show, or the actors, or even what it was about. From what I understand the actors were not prejudiced in their personal lives as they were depicted onscreen. My point is to turn a light on something else.

COMPARISONS

Comparing this show and the actions of others in different areas to things they may have believed were "right" at the time but were lacking in that they did not provide for the true freedom and equity of all people, or even those just in their own area of the world. This is because I hope to help others see in a different light what they may have totally ignored in times past, and maybe are still ignoring today.

It is my custom to compare things with what the Bible says about them, and particularly what Christ said about them. For I have observed that all too often what people *think* Christ said or meant, as well as what they *think* the Bible says or means, is not the same. In fact, quite often it is the opposite.

BY WHAT MEASURE

We've all heard about *turning the other cheek,* New Testament book of Matthew 5: 39. But how many really think to do that. This is repeated in the New Testament book of Luke 6: 29. Jesus is giving them an example of going beyond the *eye for an eye* principle (which, was to show people *as you do unto others it shall be done unto you*). This is the *Golden Rule* found in the New Testament book of Matthew 7: 12. Today we have a saying: *What goes around, comes around.* It is the exact same principle.

The Old Testament book of Proverbs 15: 1 tells us *A soft answer turns away wrath.* A *soft* answer, not the point of a sword or gun, or even harsh words.

Most people feel it is impractical to live by these words, even *if* they be the words of God. They think if you do others will walk all over you and take advantage of you. In the New Testament book of Matthew 26:52 Jesus tells Peter *Put up again your sword into its place: for all they that take the sword shall perish with the sword.* I guess we don't really think that means what it says either while we maintain our military, regardless as to what country you speak of.

We all *wish* we could do these things, if only other people would do the same. As one song goes: We keep waiting...waiting...waiting on the world to change. We want the other guy to do it first. Remember—to the other guy, *you are the other guy*!

So, the fighting goes on one way or another and we keep wondering why there is no peace. New Testament book of Romans 3: 15-17 *Their feet are swift to shed blood: destruction and misery are in their ways: And the way of peace have they not known.* The way of peace. There is a way of peace.

Every decision, every choice has an outcome and consequences. New Testament book of Luke 6: 44 *For every tree is known by his own fruit.* We need only ask what is the fruit being borne by the actions (decisions/choices), of individuals, families, and nations? Is it serving in a positive way or a negative one?

WHAT SHOULD WE DO?

The New Testament book of Romans 2: 1 *Therefore you are inexcusable, O man, whoever thou art that judgest: for wherein you judgest another, thou condemnest thyself; For thou that judgest doest the same things.* Do we have any judging going on today? We are told rather in the New Testament book of I Corinthians 11; 31 *For if we would judge ourselves, we should not be judged.*

Prejudice and bigotry are judging others for whatever reason and finding them coming up short by the standards of those doing the judging. Yet we are told in the scripture above Romans 2: 1, that those doing the judging are doing the same things as those whom they are judging. Hypocritical? You bet! Mostly done in ignorance. Absolutely! As Christ said from the cross, *Father, forgive them for they know not what they do.* New Testament book of Luke 23: 34. They thought they were doing God's will by getting rid of a heretic. The fruit has proven otherwise. They were wrong in their comparison.

THE WAY OF PEACE

There is a tool to use for peace. It is *The Way of Peace* called *The Golden Rule* found in the New Testament book of Matthew 7: 12 *Therefore all things whatsoever ye would that men should do unto you, do you even so to them: for this is the law and the prophets.*

This fulfills the intent of the law and the teachings of the prophets, all of which spoke of and prepared the way for Christ.

These are just some comparisons out of many. Examine for yourself your own thoughts, words, actions, and judgments, and see if you can find any room for improvement. New Testament book of II Corinthians 10: 12 *For we dare not make ourselves of the number, or compare ourselves with some that commend themselves: but they measuring themselves by themselves, and comparing themselves among themselves, are not wise.*

Let Christ be what you measure yourself against. It can keep you busy enough you won't have time or the desire to compare yourself with another or to judge another.

My Brother's Keeper

I recently read where another person was informed that they do not have to feel responsibility to enlighten the world or to solve all the world's problems. I began to think about this enigma, that being: we all seem to have an innate sense that we are to save the world, or at least, the part where we live.

I began to relate this to how we all tend to want to intervene and straighten out things we perceive as problems, especially in the lives of those nearest us, like family and friends, and by extension, the world. It's interesting that we all seem to feel we "know" what is best for everyone else while being unable to solve our own problems in most cases.

A DISTORTED SENSE OF JUSTICE

Unfortunately, this innate sense has become distorted to become a kind of *judge* of other people's actions and thereby deeming it our place to intervene in what we consider as *negative situations*. Little, if ever, does it seem to occur to us that we are ourselves being negative by our very judgment of those whom we consider as behaving inappropriately. The fact that we think we need to *correct* their behavior shows we consider it as "wrong" and that we are "right", and therefore in a position to judge the matter by our "standard". We feel that our desire to *rescue* someone or something from another's improper or hurtful behavior *is* the desired way to live. A way we feel will then be beneficial to all humanity by extension.

The Bible tells us in the New Testament book of Matthew 7: 1-2 *Judge not, that ye be not judged. For with what judgment ye judge, ye shall be judged: and with what measure ye mete, it shall be measured to you again.* There is a saying in this modern world: *What goes around, comes around.* This sums up nicely what is said in the scripture above as well as the *Eye for an Eye* principle given in the Old Testament. The *judging* mentioned in Matthew 7: 1 is that which carries condemnation, not a discerning. It goes on to explain in verses 3-5 *why* you should not judge (condemn). (3) *And why beholdest thou the mote that is in thy brother's eye, but considerest not the beam that is in thine own eye? (4) Or how wilt thou say to thy brother, let me pull out the mote out of thine eye; and behold, a beam is in thine own eye? (5) Thou hypocrite, first cast out the beam that is in thine own eye; and then thou shalt see clearly to cast out the mote out of thy brother's eye.*

My mother used to say, "*Sweep around your own back door before you look to sweep around mine.*" See the connection? There's a good chance that once you get the beam out of your own eye, you'll no longer even see a mote in your brother's eye.

AM I MY BROTHER'S KEEPER?

In the Old Testament book of Genesis 4: 9 *And the Lord said unto Cain, Where is Abel thy brother? And he said, I know not: Am I my brother's keeper?* Of course, he lied. He knew he had killed his brother, as did God. When it was ascertained that he had killed his own brother, the news followed that he would be *cursed* from the earth and that henceforth the earth would no longer yield up to him her strength. A fugitive and a vagabond would he be in the earth.

I think it interesting that God did not take Cain's life. Rather, he could live with the consequences of taking something he could not replace even with his own life. (The Ten Commandments... Thou shalt not kill or do no murder.)

From this account I gather that we *are* our brother's keeper, and it fits nicely with the *Golden Rule* found in the New Testament book of Matthew 7: 12 *Therefore all things whatsoever ye would that men should do to you, do ye even so to them: for this is the fulfilling of the law and the prophets.* As I repeat throughout this book, it is the fulfilling of the intent of the law and the teachings of the prophets.

In the New Testament book of Matthew 22: 36-40, paraphrased, we find the first great commandment is to *love God*, and the second is like unto it, *love your neighbor as yourself.* Of course, this requires loving yourself first before you can love your neighbor as yourself. God even tells us in the New Testament book of I John 4: 20 *If a man say, I love God, and hateth his brother, he is a liar: for he that loveth not his brother whom he hath seen, how can he love God whom he hath not seen?* And in the New Testament book of Luke 10: we find the Parable of the *Good Samaritan* that shows *everyone* is your neighbor that you are to love as yourself.

UNWORTHINESS IN ALL

Since so many of us suffer from a sense of *unworthiness* due to what we believe are our sins, we find it easier to focus on what we perceive as our brother's sins that need to be corrected (punished), rather than looking for any sense of worthiness in him. But does this make us any more righteous? Little do we realize that in punishing our neighbor or brother we are in a sense, punishing ourselves too because we feel innately that it is deserved. The only way you recognize it in your brother is because you have it too.

So long as we continue this line of thinking, we will continue to miss the boat, so to speak, of the *grace* God has bestowed upon us through our Lord Jesus Christ. We are told in the New Testament book of Hebrews 4: 16 *Let us therefore come boldly unto the throne of grace, that we may obtain mercy, and find grace to help in time of need.*

We read in the New Testament book of Galatians 2: 16 (last part) *by the works of the law shall no flesh be justified.* The law which pointed out to them their errors could not justify them as sacrifice was required for those errors, called *sin,* which means "missing the mark". The true sacrifice offered by Jesus' life and death opened the way to grace which would justify, requiring no more physical sacrifices and offerings for sin, but a life of freedom from the death penalty that the law imposed to those who believed and accepted Jesus as the Son of God and the Lamb of God offered as the Passover whose blood saves today as the blood of the Passover lamb saved those in Egypt in the Old Testament Book of Exodus chapter 12.

WE ARE ALL CONNECTED

I saw an animated movie recently that caught my attention. In it were many different species and this phrase was repeated often, "Many leaves---One tree!" It showed they knew they were all connected even though they were also individual.

We are shown that nothing lives or dies to itself. We can see this by observing nature as well as humans and animals. There is that unseen connection, *the web of life, that* keeps the balance of everything. When something or someone disturbs that balance there is a reaction. This is what happened in the case of Cain and applies to each of us as well.

We know this in our own lives because when our bodies are out of balance, we get sick. When we cause nature to become unbalanced, we have a most unpleasant reaction that affects us all in some way. We call these "natural" events, or an "act of God", and *still* do not see the connection.

We are *all* basically fugitives and vagabonds in the world. Fugitive from our own innate understanding of how it all works together because we cut ourselves off from it long ago, and we seek to escape or avoid what we feel will be the punishment we will receive if we allow ourselves to truly face it. So, we continue to move from place to place (in our knowledge or lack of it), like vagabonds, never allowing ourselves to truly settle down because we carry the same old baggage (problems), right along with us in our pilgrimage. The same beliefs and customs that do not serve us, yet we feel (or think), as Cain, that we cannot face it. Old Testament book of Genesis 4: 13 *And Cain said unto the Lord, my punishment is greater than I can bear.* In my Bible (KJV), there is a number '9' by the above sentence, and in the middle margin it reads *Or, Mine iniquity is greater than may be forgiven.* We have this tendency to think that we are such great sinners that God can never forgive us. Are we greater than God, to whom <u>all things are possible</u>? When we are told we are forgiven through faith in Jesus, do we say then that God <u>cannot</u> forgive us? I ask again, are we greater than God? Such beliefs keep us from experiencing the power of God in our lives and need to be relinquished permanently.

JUSTICE OR MERCY

Cain's words reflect an attitude. One that says God is unjust. He never repented of killing his own brother. He was unable to see the connection between his actions toward his brother and what came on him as a result of it. The same has carried over from generation to generation. In fact, we are taught that we *all* bear *original sin* due to the actions of Adam and Eve in the Garden of Eden. In other words, we are condemned from the start! How's *that* for considering God as unjust! In our society today we have people demanding "justice" for what someone has suffered due to the actions of others. But when it comes right down to it, we want "mercy" for ourselves. Can we not see the contradiction? We want others to pay for their wrongdoings, but we want understanding for our own, not punishment.

THE LAW OF ATTRACTION

Taking another look at the *Law of Attraction* and how what you do or seek to do to another can come back on you as shown in the New Testament book of Matthew 7: 3-5, read the account of *Haman* given in the Old Testament book of Esther, Chapters 3-9, who sought to destroy the Jews and was himself and his sons destroyed on the gallows he had prepared for the Jews.

Does this seem to you that maybe we *are our brother's keeper*? And that maybe, we want to make sure to keep him in love and appreciation as we would want him to keep us? You can never find real joy and peace in your life so long as you harbor negative feelings and attitudes toward your brother or neighbor, whom Jesus showed in the parable of the *Good Samaritan* you are to love as yourself. New Testament book of Luke, Chapter 10 and New Testament book of Matthew 22: 36-40.

CHRIST CONSCIOUSNESS

The question is asked in the New Testament book of Romans 2: 21-23 *Thou therefore which teachest another, teachest thou not thyself? Thou that preachest a man should not steal, dost thou steal? (22) Thou that sayest a man should not commit adultery, dost thou commit adultery? Thou that abhorrest idols, dost thou commit sacrilege? (23) Thou that makest thy boast of the law, through breaking the law dishonorest thou God?* Jesus told those wanting to stone the woman taken in adultery, *let him that is without sin among you first cast a stone at her. So,* I ask those of you who may want to condemn your brother or neighbor...are *you* without sin?

Wouldn't you rather be happy and joyful in your life? Wouldn't you really prefer to be relieved of the burden of judging others, and enlighten them instead? Aren't you glad you don't <u>really</u> have that function to fill?

Jesus told Herod, *Go and find what this means, I would have mercy and not sacrifice.* New Testament book of Matthew 9: 13. We feel much better when we unite to help one another than we do when we unite to destroy one another. There is that innate *Christ Consciousness* that reminds us it is better to love and forgive than to condemn and require a penalty, because such has a way of boomeranging right back on us.

Let us enter into the joyful, abundant life Christ said he came so that we may have it, by learning to truly love God and our neighbor as ourselves. This will leave no room for judging and condemning, as we will be too busy being *our brother's keeper.*

WHAT GOD HATH JOINED TOGETHER

I am going to be discussing a misunderstood saying of Christ in the Bible that has become an entrenched belief that causes unnecessary grief and suffering on so many levels.

Before I start, let me preface this by saying, I know many will reject what I will be saying here because it contradicts what they have believed and been taught for generations. Still, I feel it needs to be said, and hopefully, some will open the windows of their minds and allow the fresh air of understanding to clear the cobwebs of old ideas and beliefs that do not serve any longer—but rather, hinder.

For uncounted generations we have been taught *What God hath joined together let not man put asunder,* referred to marriage. Once a couple underwent the ceremony of marriage by whatever means, they were then united *until death do us part*, according to the ceremony of the wedding service.

A CLOSER LOOK

Let's start in the beginning with Adam and Eve. This will of necessity be paraphrased lest this article become a book.

God created Adam from the dust of the earth to which he would return. Old Testament book of Genesis 3: 19, (last part), as well as the Old Testament book of Ecclesiastes 9: 5 *For the living know they shall die:*

but the dead know not anything, neither have they any more a reward: for the memory of them is forgotten.

In the book of Genesis, after the creation of Eve (whom Adam named because she was to be the mother of all living), God calls Eve Adam's wife, but no ceremony is listed that God performed setting a precedent for all mankind to follow. Rather, we find that God said he would make a "helpmeet" for Adam. Old Testament book of Genesis 2: 18 *And the Lord God said, It is not good that the man should be alone; I will make him an help meet for him.* In the KJV there is a number 9 by the word *meet*, and in the middle margin it is from the Hebrew *"as before him"*. *A helper that was before him?*

God created Eve from a part of Adam (not all of him), to be a *help* that was *fit* for him. A match or mate that would supply what he now lacked since she was taken *out* from him. Before that she was *within* him, and *before him* (before he was made a physical being). Once he was created physically and the breath of life was breathed into him, animating him (as a beast is animated), both aspects were within Adam, but he physically, only represented the male aspect.

The Hebrew word *Nepes* is used for "living soul", and it is used for animal as well. So, you might say Adam was inanimate until he received the breath of life. He was not a "dead" soul, just an inanimate "being" or creature.

SYMBOLISM

It will help immensely in understanding what I am saying here if you understand *symbolism*. A symbol is: something that stands for or suggests something else by reason of relationship, association, convention, or accidental resemblance; especially: a visible sign of something invisible (the lion is a symbol of courage). This is from Merriam Webster's Deluxe Dictionary, Tenth Collegiate Edition, 2nd explanation of usage.

NEW TESTAMENT EXAMPLE

In the New Testament book of John, we have the account of Jesus speaking with the Samaritan woman at the well. John 4: 7-25. Aside from the fact that he is speaking to a Samaritan, and a woman at that (The Jews had no dealings with them because they considered them unclean), was that when Jesus told the woman to go call her husband and come to him, and she said she had no husband, he told her she had had five husbands and the one she was with then was not her husband, in this she had spoken truly saying she had no husband.

Five husbands! Did this mean she had outlived five men whom she had married, or was divorce involved? Jesus told her the one she was now with was not her husband, so she must have been living with a man at the time. Did Jesus condemn her? No. So, what was going on here?

This calls to mind another example of Jesus not condemning when he could have. This is found in the New Testament book of John 8: 1-11, the woman taken in adultery. The law was clear that such was to be stoned to death. But Jesus' intent was beyond the letter of the law and to show mercy.

A LOOK AT ISAIAH

In the Old Testament book of Isaiah 54: 5 we read, *For thy Maker is thine husband, the Lord of hosts is his name; and thy Redeemer the Holy One of Israel; the God of the whole earth shall he be called.* This does not portray a physical relationship of the type we usually think of when we think of husband and wife. Symbolic? Yes. Deeply meaningful, absolutely!

Jesus told the woman at the well, *God is Spirit.* New Testament book of John 4: 24. In the above scripture of Isaiah *God* is the *One* referred to as *thy Maker is thine husband.* Does this not refer to both male and female? Isn't it being said to Israel and by extension the whole world? Isn't God the Maker of all that is?

BACK TO GENESIS

In the Old Testament book of Genesis, we have the creation of Adam, Genesis 2:7 *And the Lord God formed man of the dust of the ground, and breathed into his nostrils the breath of life; and man became a living soul.* I covered this earlier about Adam became a living (or animated) being. Spirit joined with flesh in the creation of mankind. This is the connection of what God hath joined. Everything else comes afterward.

Remember, Eve was taken out of Adam after he received the breath of life. She was now the manifested physical part of him that he could see, be aware of; a part of his makeup he would need to be in harmony with, to truly function. What is also known as the *Yin/Yang,* balance between two opposites. (Another means of showing God is no respecter of persons.)

A TYPE OF SYMBOL

In the New Testament book of Romans 14: 17 *For the kingdom of God is not meat and drink...*Meat and drink are for the physical, to sustain life. Spirit cannot die and has no need of physical sustenance to sustain life as man does. Yet the physical is a type, a symbol of what God is doing with and through man.

WHAT ABOUT MARRIAGE?

Am I saying there is no need for marriage? Not at all. The joining of a man and woman should represent the completion of the circle of reuniting male, female, and God, their Creator, picturing when *All Was One in the beginning,* as well as fulfilling the two great commandments spoken of by Jesus is the New Testament book of Matthew 22: 36-40 (paraphrased here), *You shall love God and your neighbor as yourself.* These three in one, just as your body, mind, and spirit make up your one physical entity.

When Jesus had just explained this in the New Testament book of Matthew 19: 3-6, he was asked (7) *They say unto him, Why did Moses then command to give a writing of divorcement, and to put her away?* He saith unto them (8) *Moses because of the hardness of your hearts suffered you to put away your wives: but from the beginning it was not so. (9) And I say unto you, Whosoever shall put away his wife, except it be for fornication and shall marry another, committeth adultery: and whoso marrieth her which is put away doth commit adultery. (10) His disciples say unto him, if the case of the man be so with his wife, it is good not to marry.* But Jesus tells them in (vs 11) *All men cannot receive this saying, save they to whom it is given.* They still did not understand the spiritual principle here. So it is, still today.

Jesus told his disciples in the New Testament book of John 16: 7 *Nevertheless I tell you the truth; It is expedient for you that I go away: for if I go not away, the Comforter will not come unto you; but if I depart, I will send him unto you.* Here Jesus was promising another "helper" for man. Only *this* helper would dwell *in* them, not just *with* them as a wife might. Things were going to progress beyond the presently accepted ideas and beliefs.

It is all symbolic. In the New Testament book of Revelation 19: 7, we read, *Let us be glad and rejoice, and give honour to him: for the marriage of the Lamb is come, and his wife hath made herself ready.* And in chapter 21: 2 *And I John saw the holy city, coming down from God out of heaven, prepared as a bride adorned for her husband.*

We know that churches, cities, and lambs do not marry. It is used to symbolize something else. When a man and woman join, becoming one flesh symbolically, they are symbolizing the way it was in the beginning, when they were one with God. When they have children, they are as God to the children in that they have brought forth new life into the world by reason of their union, even as God brought forth new life in joining spirit to flesh and creating a new being.

We have repeated examples of the physical life ending at some point and the Bible speaks of the one remaining alive being able to marry again once a spouse dies.

As they, the couple joining in marriage, are representing the plan of God; there was not to be any divorce. Yet humans without the understanding of the purpose of marriage and what it typified could not with a true heart stay married if there were problems which they were unable to work out. Which is why, Moses allowed the writing of divorcement, due to the hardness of their hearts.

God is not divided, and it was not intended for a man and woman to put asunder that which God had joined, as they represented the creation of the *One*, and the ongoing creation through their children and families. We find in the New Testament book of Mark 10: 2-9 that this applied as well to women putting away their husbands.

This hardness of heart (lack of understanding) was why God allowed the kings to have multiple wives and concubines. Even then, they were not to take another man's wife as David did Bathsheba, found in the Old Testament book of II Samuel11 and 12.

After the death of their son born of adultery, Bathsheba is then called David's wife. II Samuel 12: 24, though no ceremony is given. We also have the example found in the Old Testament book of I Samuel 25:44 when King Saul took away his daughter from David and gave her to another man for wife. David later had her taken away from that man because she was *his* wife. II Samuel 3: 13-16

The man and woman together were to portray the plan of God in the flesh even as Jesus was called *Emannuel* (God with us), New Testament book of Matthew 1: 23. God is in each of us and is most appropriately exhibited in us when we live by the *Golden Rule* found in the New Testament book of Matthew 7: 12. For this is the fulfillment of the law and the prophets. Of the intent of the law and the teachings of the prophets.

IN CONCLUSION

As I said in the beginning, there will be those who will disagree with my concept here, still thinking this is about marriage and divorce. I tell you that *if* you truly understand what is pictured here, there would be no divorce and people would not enter lightly into any marriage.

Yet because it is not truly understood, we continue to have divorce and to condemn and stigmatize those who do divorce. One of the Ten Commandments is: *Thou shalt not kill (or do no murder).* While a murderer is condemned and stigmatized, killing others in war is not! Yet it is still killing and taking something, you cannot replace even with your own life.

My point is: this subject is far deeper than what I have written here. Let him who has ears to hear, hear it and do as the Bereans mentioned in the New Testament book of Acts 17: 10-12. Meanwhile, do not condemn nor stigmatize those who do divorce. God does not and you should not either. Apply the *Golden Rule*, knowing that as you judge you will be judged.

New Testament book of Matthew 9: 13 *But go ye and learn what that meaneth. I will have mercy, and not sacrifice, for I am not come to call the righteous, but sinners to repentance.*

Blind Leading the Blind

This article is regarding something on my mind one morning that was furthered by an email received from a friend on another subject.

While having breakfast that morning I was thinking on some things, particularly the plants on my patio area that seemed to be resurrecting after I thought they were dead and gone. After one of the hardest winters in memory in this area, I didn't think any of my plants survived. Yet even though I didn't pull them up or cut them back, one day I saw new life coming up from them.

DEAD OR DORMANT?

On the one hand I was delighted to see that they had stayed with me and were producing again after I thought they were gone for good. Today, though, I also see there is an opposite side to this.

While it is good to know *life* cannot be stopped, I also realized that it shows the possibility of things that we thought we were finished with and had overcome, might possibly be only lying dormant --- awaiting the right moment to spring forth with new life of its own.

I am aware that even when we pull something up by the roots the seed may still be in the soil and will come up again under the right conditions. This recalled a couple of scriptures. One is found in the New Testament book of Matthew 13: 24-30 Parable of the Sower in which we are told to *Let the wheat and tares grow together until the time of the harvest. (30).*

Another is found in the New Testament book of Romans 7:15 where the apostle Paul laments *That which I would, I do not, but the thing I hate, that I do!* So long as the wheat and tares grow together, we are susceptible to the influence which is why we need to have on the whole armor of God. New Testament book of Ephesians 6: 11. The helmet, to protect our heads where our minds and thoughts are; the shield, to protect the heart and other vital organs; and the sword of truth, to defend us from false ideas and beliefs that can wound and even destroy us but can be cut down by the sword of truth.

THE EMAIL

This brings me to the email mentioned earlier. It had to do with the political party in this country (USA), called the *Democrats,* and the appeal they were putting forth to the people, essentially blaming those with money (the wealthy), for the unhappy condition of the lives of those without the same amount of money, or even close to it.

Before you think I am a member of the opposing political party, the *Republicans*, and therefore I am accusing the Democrats here—think again. Both parties have their part in this. For either party to blame the other is for people to avoid responsibility for their own lives. It denies the freedom we each must have to make our own choices by saying another has power over us to enable or prevent us from making a choice. It also indicates that God is a respecter of persons by allowing this or approving it via whichever party is in control.

THE BLAME GAME

This has been going on since the Garden of Eden when Adam blamed Eve (really, he blamed God), because he said *the woman YOU gave to be with me, etc.* Eve blamed the serpent, and then, their son Cain saw fit to blame his brother Abel (whose offering was acceptable to God, while Cain's wasn't), as being the cause of his problems. God put the onus straightly upon Adam's shoulders. He was created first, and from what we read in the account in Genesis, Eve was deceived, but Adam wasn't. Cain had been told if he did well, he would be accepted, but if not, then sin lay at his door. In other words: he was responsible for his own actions just as Adam was.

I sent an email to my friend basically saying this same thing. That, if we Americans, or any other nationality, continue to shift the blame to anything or anyone else for the outcomes of our lives instead of taking control of our thoughts and actions (since thought always precedes action), we will continue to see ourselves as victims having no power to affect what happens in our lives. We will continue to feel instead that others have power over us (which God is allowing), and we are helpless to do anything about it. In essence, we will also be blaming God just as Adam did. But this belies the scripture found in the New Testament book of Acts 10: 34-35 *Then Peter opened his mouth, and said, Of a truth I perceive that God is no respecter of persons: (35) But in every nation he that feareth him, and worketh righteousness, is accepted with him.*

AN EMPTY RELIGION

This country, (USA), is considered a *Christian* country. What Jesus said in the Bible is very applicable to us today. *Well did Isaiah prophesy of you... these people honor me with their mouths, but their hearts are far from me.* Old Testament book of Isaiah 29: 13.

Ours is basically an empty religion, like those white-washed sepulchers mentioned by Jesus in the Bible, speaking of the Pharisees, who outwardly are beautiful, but inwardly are filled with dead men's bones and all uncleanness. New Testament book of Matthew 23: 7. The Pharisees had an outward show of righteousness, but it was a façade only as they reveled in the honor received from men and the power of their position rather than truly giving God the honor, which is why Jesus called them hypocrites. New Testament book of Matthew 23: 13-15 *But woe unto you, scribes and Pharisees, hypocrites! For you shut up the kingdom of heaven against men: for ye neither go in yourselves, neither suffer ye them that are entering to go in. (14) Woe unto you, scribes and Pharisees, hypocrites! For ye devour widows' houses, and for a pretense make long prayer: therefore ye shall receive the greater damnation. (15) Woe unto you, scribes and Pharisees, hypocrites! For ye compass sea and land to make one proselyte, and when he is made, ye make him twofold more the child of hell than yourselves.*

WHEN GOOD BECOMES EVIL

I am not condemning those programs that are there to help people, nor those who benefit from them. When God brought Israel out of Egypt and set them up as a nation representing *His Kingdom* on earth; he established three separate tithes, one of which was for this very purpose, to help those in need. The first was for the spiritual aspect of man, the second was for the mental aspect of man (where his ability to enjoy resides) and used for his pleasure physically while representing God's kingdom of abundance for all. The third was for his fellow man to show the true fulfillment of loving God and neighbor as self. New Testament book of Matthew 22: 36-40. The parable of the *Good Samaritan* found in the New Testament book of Luke 10 shows that *everyone* is your neighbor. Jesus did not condemn the poor but told his disciples, *the poor you have always, but me you have not always.* New Testament book of Matthew 26:11.

We are shown by the differences in the sacrifices and offerings found in the Old Testament book of Leviticus, that not everyone is at the same level of understanding. Yet <u>all</u> are accepted if they offer in sincerity. This being the case, we can hardly condemn anyone having need or being helped by others whose condition permits them to help.

The problem comes in when those being helped forget the true purpose of it (*you shall love your neighbor as yourself*) and start to demand help as their "right" as though they have no responsibility of their own to help themselves.

The other side of the coin are those who dispense the "help" who want to control the lives of those they are "helping" by using them for their own purpose and gain (such as political advancement), forgetting the true purpose of *you shall love your neighbor as yourself.*

CAUGHT IN A TRAP OF BLINDNESS

The same mistakes are being made repeatedly, only calling them by different names, while the blame is continually shifted back and forth, solving nothing.

Well did Jesus say, *If the blind lead the blind, shall they not both fall into the ditch?* New Testament book of Matthew 15: 14. As it is written in the New Testament book of Galatians 6: 7 *Be not deceived: God is not mocked: for whatsoever a man sows, that shall he also reap.* And in Galatians 5: 14 *For all the law is fulfilled in one word, even in this; thou shalt love thy neighbor as thyself.*

Can we not see that each side of the coin serves a purpose: one meant to show love of neighbor as self? Those in need offer opportunity to those who can help to fulfill loving thy neighbor as thyself. Each should be grateful for the opportunity the other provides. That would be going beyond the torn veil in living a *Christian* life.

THE VEIL REMAINS

The veil is still over our faces today even though the veil in the temple was torn from top to bottom in the *Holy of Holies* at the death of Christ to show the way was now open to all. We seem to prefer another human tell us which is the way we should go and what to do, and we continue to fall into the ditch, all the while claiming to be *Christians* following God's will.

The Israelites asked Moses to speak to them rather than God. Old Testament book of Exodus 20: 19. Today we have separation of church and state because we don't know how to do both together. Besides, with this system we can continue to blame other people when things don't go the way we want them to...and we dare not blame God.

In the movie *Lawrence of Arabia*, based on the life of T.E. Lawrence, Lawrence tells Sherief Ali, "So long as the Arabs fight tribe against tribe, so long will they be a little people, a silly people, greedy, barbarous and cruel... as you are." This applies to *all* people, for we all inhabit this spaceship ark called *Earth*.

Would to God we would stop condemning one another and start to really work together! We could then have the *Utopia* we all dream of no matter what our nationality, language, color, race, sex, or any other *"differences"*.

This would really be going beyond the torn veil into the glorious liberty of the children of God spoken of in the New Testament book of Romans 8: 21 *Because the creature (creation) itself also shall be delivered from the bondage of corruption into the glorious liberty (freedom) of the children of God.*

God speed the day!

Snake Handlers—True Faith or Tempting God?

This article is regarding the people called *Snake Handlers;* so-called, because they use the scripture from the New Testament book of Mark 16: 18 as their guide. This verse reads: *They shall take up serpents; and if they drink any deadly thing, it shall not hurt them. They shall lay hands upon the sick, and they shall recover.*

I started thinking about this when I read recently in the newspaper where one of their group had died from snakebite.

As part of their religious practice, some of them take up poisonous snakes to show their trust in God to keep them from harm using this scripture as *proof* to back up this practice. Yet this verse is a continuation of the preceding verse showing the signs that would follow true believers and the works they would do in Jesus' name.

PROOF OR TEMPTING

In the Bible there is the letter 's' with this scripture that refers to another scripture pertaining to this subject. That scripture is found in the New Testament book of Acts 28: 5. This gives the account of the apostle Paul being shipwrecked on the island called Melita. The barbarous people living there showed them kindness due to the rain and cold and kindled a fire for them (verses 3-5). *And when Paul had gathered a bundle of sticks and laid them on the fire, there came a viper out of the heat and fastened on his hand (4) And when the barbarians saw the venomous beast hang on his hand, they said among themselves, No doubt this man is a murderer, whom, though he hath escaped the sea, yet vengeance suffereth not to live. (5) And he shook off the beast into the fire and felt no harm. (6) Howbeit they looked when he should have swollen, or fallen down dead suddenly: but after they had looked a great while, and saw no harm come to him, they changed their minds, and said that he was a god.* Their idea being that if what they originally thought to be true wasn't—then the opposite must be true. After all, this defied the physical laws. It is well to note here that Paul did not intentionally take up the venomous snake.

JESUS' EXAMPLE

Does this mean the man that I read of who had died from snakebite was a murderer, or guilty of some other sin, or lacking in faith? Why was he not protected as promised, or healed when he was bitten?

Jesus, while being tempted by Satan, told him in the New Testament book of Matthew 4: 7 *Then Jesus said unto him, it is written again, Thou shalt not tempt the Lord thy God.* This is quoted from the Old Testament book of Deuteronomy 16: 6 *You shall not tempt the Lord thy God, as you tempted him in Massah.*

We are told in the New Testament book of James 1: 13 *Let no man say when he is tempted, I am tempted of God; for God cannot be tempted with evil, neither tempteth he any man.* God does not tempt anyone, which is a direct fulfillment of the *Golden Rule* of not doing to any something you would not want done to yourself. We are told this in the New Testament book of Matthew 7: 12 *Therefore all things whatsoever ye would that men should do to you, do ye even so to them: for this is the law and the prophets.* The fulfilling of the law and the prophets.

WHAT IS THE INTENT?

I think the intent of the scripture shows that <u>if</u> any <u>inadvertently</u> took up something like a poisonous snake, or drank something poisonous, they would be protected. To do this deliberately is to challenge God to do as he said when he said they would be protected. Rather than showing faith in God, it does the exact opposite. It requires God to keep *proving* himself to them. Satan tried this in the temptation of Jesus found in the New Testament book of Matthew 4: 5-7 *Then the devil taketh him up into the holy city, and setteth him on a pinnacle of the temple, (6) And saith unto him, If thou be the Son of God, cast thyself down: for it is written, He shall give his angels charge concerning thee: and in their hands they shall bear thee up, lest at any time thou dash thy foot against a stone. (7) Jesus said unto him, It is written again, Thou shalt not tempt the Lord thy God.* This is when Jesus quoted the scripture about tempting God.

It should be obvious that it is not needed or desired, that one put his life in mortal danger to *show* their belief that God will protect them from death by deliberately taking up deadly serpents or drinking deadly drinks to show "obedience".

Jesus did not succumb to Satan's challenge. He *knew* he was the Son of God and had no need to *prove* it by any means or to anyone, such as the malefactor who was crucified with him, and railed on him found in the New Testament book of Luke 23: 39 *And one of the malefactors which were hanged railed on him, saying, If thou be Christ, save thyself and us.*

These are other signs Jesus said would follow those who were true believers after he returned to his Father: *They shall cast out devils, they shall speak with new tongues; they shall lay hands upon the sick, and they shall recover.* None of these included doing something to deliberately put their life in danger. He also said to believe him for the very works sake. His birth, life, works, death and resurrection, all taking place according to scripture, would be enough *proof.*

GREATER WORKS

What could be considered greater works than what Jesus did? He healed all manner of sickness and disease. He fed the hungry and raised the dead. He caused the blind to see, the deaf to hear, the lame to walk, and the mute to speak.

When we come to see that the teaching of Jesus offers a means to move beyond the commonly accepted beliefs about life to an even greater understanding of the spiritual, we can begin to see how Jesus would say that to his followers. We already have a belief that the spiritual is greater than the physical by our very belief in a higher power (God). But to see how greater works than those done by Jesus can be/are being done today requires going beyond the torn veil to knowledge that includes the physical while going beyond it.

YOU REAP WHAT YOU SOW

Today we have the biblical example of Jesus as well as of Moses and the prophets. We have plenty of examples in scripture as well as everyday life to teach us that we reap what we sow. New Testament book of Galatians 6: 7 *Be not deceived: for God is not mocked: for whatsoever a man soweth, that shall he also reap.*

We have plenty of examples to show us what to avoid so we won't have so much *unwanted results* in our lives. All the examples of Jesus dealt with correcting the unwanted in people's lives. Even feeding the multitudes. No one wants to remain hungry. Yet Jesus once told his disciples *I have meat to eat you know not of.* They, thinking physically, wondered if anyone had brought him food. This is found in the New Testament book of John 4: 32-33. In Verse 34 Jesus explains to them what he meant. *Jesus saith unto them, My meat is to do the will of him that sent me, and to finish his work.* This is obviously not speaking of physical food. All the examples of the works Jesus did were things that helped people physically while trying to teach them spiritual principles that go beyond the physical. In other words: there is more to life than eating, drinking, marrying, and giving in marriage. We are all more than just our physical bodies, though that is where our primary focus tends to be.

WHAT IS MY EXAMPLE?

It would profit us to examine our own lives to see if we may be misunderstanding some of the tenets of the Bible and bringing on ourselves things that can cause our destruction. God, who tempts no man, would never require the kind of "proof" allegedly being exhibited by those referred to as *Snake Handlers* to show him or anyone else their belief in him.

In the Old Testament book of Exodus 7: 8-12 We find the account of Moses and Aaron before Pharaoh. God knew Pharaoh would want to see a miracle (vs 9). Moses and Aaron followed God's instructions and Aaron cast his rod down before Pharaoh and it became a serpent. Verse 11 *Then Pharaoh called the wise men and the sorcerers: now the magicians of Egypt,* they *also did in like manner with their enchantments. (12) For they cast down every man his rod, and they became serpents: but Aaron's rod swallowed up their rods.* This showed to Pharaoh as well as the palace magicians that the power of God that was with Moses and Aaron was greater than all theirs combined.

In the New Testament book of Acts 8: 9-21 we find the account of one Simon Magus. (Master Magician), who was a sorcerer who had bewitched the people for a long time, giving out that himself was some great one. He had a conversion that turned out to be short lived. For when he tried to get Peter and John to sell him the power to lay hands on people and have them receive the holy spirit, Peter said (20) *but Peter said unto him, Thy money perish with thee, because thou hast thought that the gift of God may be purchased with money.*

ALL POWER

The power of God is NOT a plaything to be used for someone's ego embellishment.

In the New Testament book of Matthew 28: 18 Jesus tells his disciples after his death and resurrection, *All power is given unto me in heaven and in earth.* ALL power! That means nothing is left out. He never resorted to anything that would diminish God's power in the eyes of the people, even telling Pilate *You could have no power over me except it be given you of my Father.* He refused Herod when he wanted him to "perform" for his entertainment.

The power of God is so much greater than we have understood and is not to be used in any way other than to help our fellow souls, and to honor and glorify God, the Source of the power and of everything else.

It was not denied that the sorcerers and magicians had power to do things, but they used it for their own purposes and gain and was not able to withstand the power of God, which is to be used only for good.

Hopefully, we can now see how unnecessary is behavior such as handling poisonous snakes to show our faith and trust in God. No such display is needed or even helpful. What would be helpful is for people to use the power of God to bring about true change in their own lives as well as the lives of others.

Jesus said the Father is more willing to give us of his spirit than we are to feed our own children. New Testament book of Luke 11: 13 *If ye then, being evil, know how to give good gifts unto your children: how much more shall your heavenly Father give the Holy Spirit unto them that ask him?* Have you asked? Have you received, and, if so, is it making a difference in your life? Can others see you and know that you are different from what they knew before? If not, perhaps it is time to *renew/activate* the Spirit within you that will set you apart without the need for *theatrics* such as described in this article.

THINK ABOUT IT!

THE TEN COMMANDMENTS
SEEN IN A DIFFERENT LIGHT

This is a subject that can produce different responses and/or reactions according to whomever you are speaking with about them. There are those who believe you should live by every word of the Bible, *literally*. In this modern age I realize there are those who think this is crazy as they see no way the old teachings are relevant to today's living. In this writing I will offer a different perspective on the *Decalogue*, better known as *The Ten Commandments*. While there are ten, I will divide them into four and six. My reason for this will be clear as you read on.

FIRST SOME BACKGROUND

Most people are familiar with the story of *The Ten Commandments*, either from reading it in the Bible, their religious background, or seeing the movie by Cecil B. DeMille in which actor Charlton Heston played the part of Moses, and the great scene of the parting of the Red Sea. They are aware that the Children of Israel were delivered from bondage to the Egyptians by Moses at God's command and instructions as well as all the plagues that preceded their deliverance. The story is found in the Old Testament book of Exodus.

Most people are aware that Israel is called the *chosen people of God*. However, they were not the chosen people until they were brought out of

Egypt and set up to be a nation that lived by God's laws as an example to the nations around them of *God's Kingdom on Earth.*

FURTHER BACKGROUND

To start with, God was fulfilling a promise to Abraham found in Genesis 12: 1-3 *Now the Lord had said to Abram, Get thee out of thy country, and from thy kindred, and from thy father's house, unto a land that I will shew thee: (2) And I will make of thee a great nation, and I will bless thee, and make thy name great; and thou shalt be a blessing: (3) And I will bless them that bless thee, and curse him that curseth thee: and in thee shall all families of the earth be blessed.* Abram, whose name was changed to Abraham, is called the *Father of the Faithful*, because he didn't just believe *in* God, he <u>believed</u> God. So, God was going to use his offspring in a special way because of the righteousness of Abraham and God's promise to him—not because of any righteousness of theirs. We are told in the New Testament book of Acts 10: 34 *Then Peter opened his mouth and said, Of a truth I perceive that God is no respecter of persons.*

And in the New Testament book of Ephesians 6: 9 *And, ye masters, do the same unto them, forebearing threatening: knowing that your Master also is in heaven, neither is there respect of persons with him.* Since we are told that God is no respecter of persons it is important that we understand that for God to choose someone or something for any purpose is for it or them to represent something other than that thing or themselves.

BACK TO ISRAEL BECOMING GOD'S NATION

When the people agreed to keep the covenant made by God with them, they then entered a special relationship with God whereby God would do certain things for them if they were faithful in keeping the covenant set and agreed upon by both. This was a contract, like marriage. In fact, God tells them in the Old Testament book of Jeremiah 31: 31-34 of the new covenant he will make with Israel and Judah, because they broke the old covenant even though he was as an husband to them. He mentions Israel and Judah because there were twelve tribes of Israel of which Judah was only one. However, after the split when the ten tribes went into captivity and became known as the *lost tribes*, or the *Diaspora*, that left Judah and Levi, and parts of Benjamin to become known as the Israelites. Most people tend to think only the Jews are the Israelites, and God's chosen people. The real story would fill another book. But that is not the purpose of this writing.

PLATFORM FOR A NEW PERSPECTIVE

We know there are two testaments in the Bible, Old and New, and those who hold to the *Christian* doctrine feel the New takes precedent over the Old because it relates to the birth, life, works, death, and resurrection of *Jesus called Christ, and the Son of God,* promised in the Old Testament to come and deliver his people. There are those who believe there is no longer any need to keep the ten commandments since Jesus came to set up a new religion and way of life.

However, to throw away the Old Testament now that we have the New would be a mistake that could keep mankind in ignorance of the greater intent of the plan of God. It is my desire in this writing to show the continuity of the Old and the New as well as a new perspective on them that we may not have previously considered. I wish to *expand* upon them and their meaning just as Jesus did in and by his life. They work together, one building upon the other, and going forth to even more possible understanding and continued building as more and more is understood in a new light.

With that background, let me proceed with The Ten Commandments Seen in a Different Light. All of these are found in the Old Testament book of Exodus 20: 1-17.

THE FIRST FOUR

FIRST: We are told to have no other God before the One doing the speaking. *And God spake all these words, saying, (2) I am the Lord thy God, which have brought thee out of the land of Egypt, out of the house of bondage.*

(3) Thou shalt have no other gods before me. Interesting that they are not forbidden other gods, only none before or in place of, greater than, the One doing the speaking. An example of this might be where Moses, on the advice of his father-in-law, set others below him to deal with certain problems the people brought to be solved or ruled on. But when it was brought to Moses, his decision was final.

SECOND: *(4) Thou shalt not make unto thee any graven image, or any likeness of anything that is in heaven above, or that is in the earth beneath, or that is in the water under the earth. (5) Thou shalt not bow down thyself to them, nor serve them:* In other words, like the first, we are to have no other gods. Jesus tells us in the New Testament book of John 4: 24 *God is a Spirit: and they that worship him must worship him in spirit and in truth.* We should not think anything that has been created of the physical is God as God is God. No birds or flying creatures, no cattle or other beasts, no water creatures of any sort are to be bowed down to or worshipped, and certainly, no human being either.

Mankind was made in the image of God. Old Testament book of Genesis 1: 26-27 *And God said, Let us make man in our image, after our likeness: and let them have dominion over the fish of the sea, and over the fowl of the air, and over the cattle, and over all the earth, and over every creeping thing that creepeth upon the earth. (27) So God created man in his own image, in the image of God created he him, Male and female created he them.* Yet, man was not to be bowed down to and worshipped either, but was rather, given dominion over the earth as a type of the true God who has dominion over all. A physical creation representative of the Spirit God, having also the spirit of God in him, setting him apart from all the rest of creation. New Testament book of Romans 8: 16 *The Spirit itself bears witness with our spirit, that we are the children of God:*

All my life, and that of most others that I know, we have had the tendency to think of the ten commandments in the negative: *Thou shalt not!* If God had said *Thou shalt be extremely happy,* I wonder if we would have believed God. Yet the key to our happiness lies in a better understanding of these things and what they were intended to represent. In the Old Testament book of Proverbs 4: 7, we read, *Wisdom is the principal thing; therefore get wisdom: and with all thy getting get understanding.* For it is only with understanding that you will be able to see beyond the previously accepted beliefs about the commandments, the holy days, the sacrifices, offerings, prophecies, and everything else given to the people from the beginning of their being set up as God's nation.

THIRD: We are told in vs7 *Thou shalt not take the name of the Lord thy God in vain...*There is meaning in a name which is why names were changed to show the significance of what they represented. Abram was changed to Abraham, Sarai was changed to Sarah, and Jacob was changed to Israel. Cephas was changed to Peter and Saul was changed to Paul. These name changes are from the Old and New Testaments.

In the New Testament book of John 16: 24 Jesus told his disciples *Hitherto have ye asked nothing in my name: ask, that ye may receive, that your joy may be full.* There was power in using Jesus' name. There is even the account of one using Jesus' name and casting out devils even though he was not part of the group of twelve disciples. New Testament book of Mark 9: 38-39 *And John answered him, saying, Master, we saw one casting out devils in thy name, and we forbad him, because he followeth not us.* Jesus replies (39) *Forbid him not; for there is no man which shall do a miracle in my name, that can lightly speak evil of me. (40) For he that is not against us is on our part.* This man, whoever he was, recognized the power in Jesus' name and used it for good...not in vain or empty self-promoting way. Even more reason not to use God's name in a vain, irreverent, puny or powerless way. Not because of some feared punishment that may come upon us; but because we are denying the very power that is in us also as the offspring of God! It is because of our lack of understanding of this that we continue to miss the boat (or ark, if you will), and in so doing we have denied ourselves much joy and happiness that could be ours; not to mention the power that is available to us.

FOURTH: Now we come to the Sabbath commandment which I personally feel we have misunderstood for...like, forever? Verse 8 *Remember the sabbath day to keep it holy. (9-11) Six days shalt thou labor and do all thy work: but the seventh day is the sabbath of the Lord thy God: in it thou shalt not do any work, thou, nor thy son, nor thy daughter, thy manservant, nor thy maidservant, thy cattle, nor any stranger that is within thy gates: for in six days the Lord made heaven and the earth, the sea, and all that in them is, and rested the seventh day: wherefore the Lord blessed the seventh day, and hallowed it.*

In the first place you can only remember something if you knew it before, and only God, the non-physical Source of All-That-Is, can make anything *holy*. The Sabbath was to be a reminder. The Sabbath was given to them as a time of rest that pictured God's kingdom on earth when all their needs would be provided for them and there would be no need for them or any of their family, servants or cattle to do the labor they had to do physically to survive. As offspring of God, they had experienced this before coming into the earth plane of existence. Therefore, they were told to remember.

But mankind tends to view everything through the lens of the physical, so he latched onto the physical aspects: *Six days shalt thou labor and do all thy works, but the seventh day is the rest of the Lord thy God...*It was to picture the rest that would be for all people in God's kingdom, and they were even told the stranger within thy gates was to do no labor, showing this was for *all,* not just the people of Israel.

So many rules and regulations have been attached to this commandment in man's attempt to try to *enforce* keeping the day holy physically, that many have been turned off by the whole thing. Yet Jesus told the people in the New Testament book of Matthew 12: 8 *For the Son of man is Lord even of the sabbath day.*

He had just finished recounting to them when David and his men went into the house of God and ate the shewbread because they were hungry, which was not lawful for them to eat, but the priests only. New Testament book of Matthew 12: 3-4. Could it be that David had a better spiritual understanding of what it represented physically, so he was not hesitant to use it to satisfy his hunger. Could this be why God called David *a man after mine own heart,* because he was able to see beyond just the physical intent? David was also a man that owned up to his deeds when it was brought to his attention. He did not try to justify or shift the blame to another. He took responsibility for his own actions, which no doubt was pleasing in God's eyes, and perhaps why God said he would never lack for a descendent to sit on the throne of Israel.

THE OTHER SIX

FIFTH: The fifth is called the first commandment with promise. (12) *Honor thy father and thy mother: that thy days may be long in the land the Lord thy God giveth thee.* Your parents are your first physical representatives of God for you. (For some this is a caregiver who is not the biological parent.) You are not given the prerogative to decide whether *you think they are honorable.* You are told to honor them (for the position they hold). They are your physical progenitor as God is your Spiritual progenitor. New Testament book of Matthew 23: 9 *And call no man your father upon the earth: for one is your Father, which is in heaven. (Notice the difference between the lower-case father, and the capitalized Father.)* This is referring to the *One God of Spirit as opposed to the physical father.* Do not refer to another physical human being as your *Spiritual Father.* As Jesus sent word to his followers after his resurrection, New Testament book of John 20: 17 *Jesus saith unto her, touch me not; for I have not yet ascended to my Father: but go to my brethren, and say unto them, I ascend unto my Father, and your Father; and to my God, and your God.* Here Jesus shows our true progenitor. We are to honor our physical father and mother—but not before or in place of God.

Therefore, the first of the last six commandments deals with your parents, whom you are an extension of, just as the first deals with God, the Source of all life, to whom all honor belongs, and of whom we are all extensions. New Testament book of Acts 17: 28 *For in him we live, and move, and have our being: as certain also of your own poets have said, For we are also his offspring.*

SIXTH: The sixth commandment is (13) *Thou shalt not kill.* This is better rendered *thou shalt do no murder.* Because we kill to eat (even plants and fruit). As this applies to the physical is obvious as you can never harm or hurt in any way the non-physical or spirit.

It's a safe assumption that it's referring to your fellow man. We can see how this is bound up with the rest of the commandments: By taking someone's life you are taking something that is not yours (8ᵗʰ) and cannot be replaced with your own. You are breaking the (1ˢᵗ) by having your own

---

will in place of God's (to whom all belong), therefore setting yourself before God. In breaking the first, all the rest fall as they are all based on the first.

I think we can see what a *ball of wax* this one is as everyone tries to figure out why it's "okay" under certain circumstances to put to death a fellow human being. Again, we are putting ourselves in the place of God and judging whether another deserves to live or die. I know there will be those who will remind me that the Old Testament says, 'such and such'. Do we still not understand that the law was given to try to teach them *how* to love God and their neighbor as themselves as Jesus explained in the New Testament book of Matthew 22: 36-40 (called the Two Great Commandments). *Master, what is the great commandment in the law? (37) Jesus said unto him, Thou shalt love the Lord thy God with all thy heart, with all thy soul, and with all thy mind. (38) This is the first and great commandment. (39) And the second is like unto it, Thou shalt love thy neighbor as thyself. (40) On these two commandments hang all the law and the prophets.* The physical punishment they received was to teach them what they did not want to receive and would not be happy with the results of whatever act brought it on. As physical beings they could relate to pain, discomfort, and fear. The sad part is that we never seem to get past the physical to the spiritual intent. So, people continue to break the laws and sin (which means missing the mark you were aiming for), which they then try to alleviate the guilt of by sacrifices and offerings, or even pointing the finger at someone else as their excuse.

SEVENTH: The seventh is (14) *Thou shalt not commit adultery.* Probably no other commandment being broken can incite the breaking of the sixth like the breaking of this one. First let me state that adultery is more than just sexual. Cooks and chemists know this, as adding anything to the original adulterates it and it is no longer pure. It changes it. It no longer has the strength of the original. So, you might say Adam and Eve committed *spiritual adultery* when they listened to the serpent and then ate of the tree of the knowledge of good and evil. They were no longer *pure* in the knowledge of God by partaking of *good and evil.* They were then forbidden to take of the Tree of Life and live forever in a condition of confusion, of wanted and unwanted, of the potential of destroying themselves and others.

Of all we humans experience we seem to take the greatest issue with sexuality. I suppose it shouldn't be surprising since we owe our very existence on this physical plane to the sexual act. And we have also made a 'god' out of this ability to procreate. We want to say who can and can't, who should or shouldn't, and how and when and under what circumstances it is to take place...if at all! People will quicker kill you for adultery than for say...dishonoring your parents.

In the New Testament book of John 8: 3-7, a woman is brought before Jesus to try to catch him with the law. Here was a woman caught in the very act of adultery. Now this means there had to have been a man too, but he seems to have escaped them.

Also, they had to have knowledge that this was going on for them to catch them in the very act. How is it they did not know they were guilty by association since they had not reported it before when they knew about it? They tried to throw the law in his face so they would have something to accuse him with for disobeying or talking against the law. The penalty for adultery was stoning, and here was a woman taken in the very act. But Jesus was not taken in by them. He said, (7) *So when they continued asking him, he lifteth up himself, and said unto them, He that is without sin among you, let him first cast a stone at her.* They knew they could not claim to be without sin, or they would be liable themselves for blasphemy, so they left, beginning with the oldest. Jesus was the only one there who was without sin and would have been within his right to stone her according to the law. Instead, he did not condemn her but told her to go and sin no more.

If killing people truly kept others from breaking the law, why do we still have the death penalty today? Killing has never stopped people from sinning and never will.

Jesus said in the New Testament book of Matthew 12: 7 *But if ye had known what this means, I would have mercy and not sacrifice, ye would not have condemned the guiltless.* They would have understood that it symbolized something greater than what they understood as the physical punishment for breaking the law. And it is so with all the laws God gave them. He was not saying the woman was guiltless, but this is a reference to himself and what they would do to him who was guiltless because of their ignorance and lack of understanding of the purpose of the law.

EIGHTH: The eighth commandment is (15) *Thou shalt not steal.* To take anything belonging to another is stealing. Thus, the sixth commandment on killing and the seventh on adultery are forms of stealing. In today's modern world we have all heard of *Identity Theft.* To steal another's identity is the same as killing him. You claim their life is yours when you take their identity. You destroy their reputation, their livelihood, and in some cases, even their life, when they can't live with the problems you have created—all without laying a finger on them. Gossip is another way of stealing a person's reputation and is just as deadly as murder. It is tied in with the 9th on false witness.

In the Old Testament book of Haggai 2:8 *The silver is mine, and the gold is mine, saith the Lord of hosts.* Since it all belongs to God, when you steal from another you are in effect stealing from God. You will also be breaking the *Golden Rule*, which sums up all the commandments, laws, rules, days, sacrifices, etc., given to the children of Israel to teach them how to love God and neighbor as self.

NINTH: The ninth commandment is (16) *Thou shalt not bear false witness against thy neighbor.* Can we see how this is abused today causing no end of heartache and misery? Can we see how lives are destroyed, sometimes causing people to take their own lives because they cannot live with the pain and humiliation caused by *false witness.*

Can we see how *false advertising* and marketing products *falsely* can create problems for people—and has—and does. Can we not see that withholding the truth is the same as lying and bearing false witness? There is no such thing as a *little white lie.* A lie is a lie and colors have nothing to do with it. It gets into intention. It gets into this as mentioned in the eighth...you are lying to God who owns all things and all souls. No wonder we are told in the New Testament book of Matthew 5: 37 *But let your communication be Yea, yea, Nay, nay: for whatsoever is more than these cometh of evil.* Remember the Golden Rule is to do unto others as you would have them do unto you. No one wants to be lied about or to...so don't do it to someone else.

TENTH: The tenth is (17) *Thou shalt not covet thy neighbor's house, thou shalt not covet thy neighbor's wife, nor his manservant, nor his maidservant, nor his ox, nor his ass, nor anything that is thy neighbor's.* And in case you aren't sure who your neighbor is: read the New Testament book of Luke 10: 30-37, the parable of the Good Samaritan, which shows <u>everyone</u> is your neighbor. So, you are not to covet (inordinately desire or lust after), anything of anyone else since everyone is your neighbor.

Lust and coveting are in the mind. If allowed free range they will bring forth action toward what is being coveted or lusted after. You really don't want your neighbor lusting or coveting after what you have either. Part of the reason we don't have peace in the world, or our lives is the breaking of this commandment. Sooner or later people will do more than lust. They will take action that usually ends in an unhappy situation for someone. To quote from the protagonist *Tevye* in the movie *A Fiddler on the Roof,* "An eye for an eye, and a tooth for a tooth. Very good! That way the whole world can be blind and toothless!" This alone, should help us see that the rules were for more than punishing people who broke them. They were for teaching them to treat others the way they wanted others to treat them. There is a saying in modern terms: *what goes around comes around.* This perfectly sums up what is said in the New Testament book of Galatians 6: 7 *Be not deceived: God is not mocked: for whatsoever a man soweth, that shall he also reap.*

Realize there is more to the Ten Commandments than you may have previously thought, and that both the Old and New Testaments work together to show an expanded way of living as people grow in spiritual understanding that was intended from the start. Therefore, Christ came: to show the people that God is *Love* and his laws *love.* God is not some tyrant who can't wait to smash you for the least offence of being human after he made you that way; and even wants you to destroy others to please him. God is Love and God is Creator, not destroyer.

Imagine a world, or even a village, where everyone treated everyone else the way they wanted to be treated themselves: with love and respect, doing nothing that would harm another in any way because you do not want another harming you in any way. This is the judging spoken of in the New Testament book of I Corinthians 11: 31 *But if we would judge ourselves, we should not be judged.*

In the New Testament book of Romans 7:14 *For we know the law is spiritual*...and in Romans 8: 5 *For they that are after the flesh do mind the things of the flesh; but they that are after the Spirit the things of the Spirit.* And in Romans 10: 4 *For Christ is the end of the law for righteousness to everyone that believeth.* Christ is the result, the fulfillment of the law in its intended form. And as we are then told in the New Testament book of Galatians 5: 22-23 *But the fruit of the Spirit is love, joy, peace, longsuffering, gentleness, goodness, faith, meekness, temperance: against such there is no law.*

IN SUMMARY

There we have it. The actions taken by those who break the law and its results that end in death, and the fruit of the Spirit which fulfills the intent of the law, bringing only good feelings and wanted things, and against which there can be no law of any kind.

To sum up: the first four teach us how to love God and the last six teach us how to love our neighbor as ourselves as said in the two great commandments Jesus quoted in the New Testament book of Matthew 22: 36-40. He also said a *new* commandment I give you, *that you love one another as I have loved you* and *by this shall all men know you are my disciples, if you have love one to another.* New Testament book of John 13: 34-35.

THE 21ST CENTURY WOMAN
OF PROVERBS 31

I'm sure women of many generations shuddered every time Mother's Day was coming up because they knew they would hear about the *Proverbs 31 Woman*. At least those of the Christian persuasion. I know those who attended the church I did certainly heard it.

We would be told how wonderful this woman was and she would be used as a mirror for us to reflect on and compare ourselves with leaving most of us feeling hopelessly incompetent and inadequate with little hope of ever achieving such a status as the woman of Proverbs 31. I used to wonder why there was no Proverbs 31 man, as it seemed to me at the time women were mostly portrayed in a negative light---always having to strive to reach a higher level of recognition while maintaining a reputation that would keep the man, or her husband, in a place of honor that was *rightfully his just by virtue of being born male.*

A NEW CONTEXT

Now I am going to speak about the Proverbs 31 woman, but in context of the 21st century in which we find ourselves. I think we can see some things differently, and we will do so without having to put down men just so we can make ourselves as women look better. That approach would only be transferring the burden from one to the other. And truly, there is no burden other than the one we have all participated in for generations—the burden of *ignorance,* too often—*willfully ignorant.*

I will begin by quoting from the King James Bible (KJV), Old Testament, Proverbs 31: 10-31 *Who can find a virtuous woman? For her price is far above rubies. The heart of her husband doth safely trust in her, so that he shall have no need of spoil. She will do him good and not evil all the days of her life. She seeks wool and flax and works willingly with her hands. She is like the merchant's ships. She brings her food from afar. She rises also while it is yet night and giveth meat to her household, and a portion to her maidens. She considereth a field and buyeth it: with the fruit of her hands she plants a vineyard. She girdeth her loins with strength, and strengthens her arms. She perceiveth that her merchandise is good. Her candle goeth not out by night. She lays her hands to the spindle and her hands hold the distaff. She stretches out her hand to the poor, yea, she reacheth forth her hand to the needy. She is not afraid of the snow for her household: For all her household are clothed with scarlet. She maketh herself coverings of tapestry; her clothing is silk and purple. Her husband is known in the gates when he sits among the elders of the land. She maketh fine linen and sells it; and delivers girdles to the merchant. Strength and honor are her clothing; and she shall rejoice in time to come. She opens her mouth with wisdom; and in her tongue is the law of kindness. She looketh well to the ways of her household, and eats not the bread of idleness. Her children rise up and call her blessed; her husband also, and he praiseth her.*

Many daughters have done virtuously, but you have excelled them all. Favor is deceitful and beauty is vain: but the woman who feareth the Lord, she shall be praised. Give her of the fruit of her hands; and let her own works praise her in the gates.

It says her husband's heart doth safely trust in her so that he hath no need of spoil. He doesn't have to have spoil because she is not continuously wanting and expecting more than he can provide for her, and, as we shall see, this woman is very capable in her own right.

Consider the statement, *her price is far above rubies.* At the time of this writing jewels and metals such as gold and silver were of great value, as were gems of various types, as they still are today. Here is a woman who was far more valuable than precious jewels. Men went for the spoils of war such as these and often brought them to their women to honor and please them as well as to win their admiration for their husband's ability to bring them to her. Men today still buy jewelry to please, honor, and win the admiration of women.

But this woman's husband had no need of spoil. Remember: *the spoils of war* meant there *was war*! This meant fighting and other dangerous activity in which the possibility of the man not returning home was always current. Whether wars or raids, these *spoils* were things that belonged to another and were taken from them, maybe along with their life. This man had no need of such as he had a woman in whom his heart safely trusts. He had no need to take something away from another whether by *right of victor*, or any other reason. You might say, because of the character of his wife, he was able to abide by the *Golden Rule* found in the New Testament book of Matthew 7: 12 *Therefore, all things whatsoever ye would that men should do to you, do ye even so to them: for this is the law and the prophets. (She will do him good and not evil all the days of her life.)*

She seeks wool and flax and works willingly with her hands. She *seeks* wool and flax. In modern terminology, she goes to the stores and vendors that sell the materials she needs to work with. With today's computer technology she may even go on-line and research the best deals to save time and expense of running all over the place looking.

She is like the merchant's ships. She brings her food from afar. Again, in modern terms, she seeks the best for her family and often brings it from afar because we are not set up primarily as an agrarian society today. We have farms and farmers, but by and large, most people live in or near towns and cities. She may even order her food on-line to be sent from afar like the merchant's ships.

She riseth while it is yet night and giveth meat to her household and a portion to her maidens. Here is a woman who gets up before daylight, (or early, in modern terminology), to oversee her household, making sure they get fed their breakfast, including her maidens (or servants). Today these could include live-in servants, housekeepers, maids, those hired to baby-sit, clean, tutor, etc. She sets the example and makes sure those under her domain are cared for.

She considereth a field and buyeth it. In modern terminology she is into real estate. It says *she buyeth it.* It doesn't say she asks her husband if she can have it or to buy it for her. *With the fruit of her hands she plants a vineyard.* Here in modern terms is a woman who has knowledge of gardening, farming, vineyard growing and harvesting. A vineyard takes room, more room than a garden plot. (Maybe this is why she buys the field?) I hardly think she does all the manual labor herself. It says with the fruit of her hands. She has the money and finances to. buy the field, perhaps even from her other endeavors. She would no doubt hire workers to do the manual labor, making her an *employer* too.

She girdeth her loins with strength, and strengthens her arms. In modern terms we might say she goes to the gym or health club to *work out.*

A HUMOROUS NOTE

After reading of all this woman does, *if she actually did it all herself,* she wouldn't be around for long because she would work herself to death. And by never sleeping, couldn't possibly last long along with all that work. This alone, should tell us there is more to this than what is generally taken from it.

BACK TO THE PROVERBS 31 WOMAN

She perceiveth that her merchandise is good. She is a businesswoman! Doesn't that fit right in with today's modern woman? *Her candle goeth not out by night.* Rather than not sleeping, this shows the woman is able to work any time of the day or night. In modern society this is especially true as we have some businesses that are on a 24-hour schedule.

She is not lazy. She is diligent. *She lays her hands to the spindle and her hands hold the distaff.* In modern terms she might be in the fabric or clothing industry.

She stretcheth out her hand to the poor, yea, she reacheth forth her hand to the needy. In modern terms she is into charity work. This covers a broad spectrum, including volunteering.

She is not afraid of the snow for her household: for all her household are clothed with scarlet. Remember, all her household included her maidens or servants. She even makes certain they are well provided for (today's salaries?). After all, as part of her household they are representative of her just as today's workers represent their employers and the companies they work for. *She maketh herself coverings of tapestry, her clothing is silk and purple.* In modern terms you might say she is into high fashion and dresses in the finest there is available.

To those who think they have no servants: consider your many appliances and devices that do the work for you freeing your time for other endeavors. They also have to be maintained and cared for just as the woman's maidens did.

Her husband is known in the gates when he sits with the elders of the land. Interesting. He is *known*. Perhaps because he is *her* husband! So often we hear, "Oh, she's the wife of So and So." Here is a man who is known because of his wife. *Her husband is known... With all the activities and abilities of this woman her husband couldn't help but be known!*

She maketh fine linen and sells it; and delivereth girdles to the merchant. Here in modern terms is a woman who is an entrepreneur. She maketh fine linen. She may even have a factory in order to make enough to deliver girdles to the merchant. She is into marketing. Since the merchants often had ships that brought things from afar, they no doubt take her merchandise afar too, showing she is also into shipping and distribution.

Strength and honor are her clothing. She is surrounded by a reputation for dealing honorably with strength of purpose. This is not talking of her physical clothing which we have already discussed. *She shall rejoice in time to come.* She knows things take time and that, in the fulness of time she will rejoice in the fruit of her labors. *She opens her mouth with wisdom and in her tongue is the law of kindness.* Besides all her physical and material works, she is also spiritual in her character. *She looketh well to the ways of her household and eats not the bread of idleness.* She makes certain her household is run properly and smoothly, as I am sure she does for her other businesses. She sets the example of getting things done because she understands *she will reap what she sows.* New Testament book of Galatians 6:7 *Be not deceived; God is not mocked: for whatsoever a man soweth, that shall he also reap.*

Her children rise up and call her blessed, her husband also, and he praiseth her. In the time this was written it was the custom for people to stand up when an elder entered the room. Here we find not only her children rising up to greet her as one would an elder, but her husband too, and he praiseth her. No doubt he is her elder (as was the custom in those days), but he honors her as his elder. He acknowledges the magnificent woman he has as his wife. What a difference it would make today if men would praise their wives instead of focusing on their supposed faults and shortcomings. This applies to women as well, to praise their husbands rather than focusing on their supposed faults and shortcomings. I am always impressed by a man or a woman upholding their mate—especially when that mate is not around to hear it.

Many daughters have done virtuously... (the Bible has the number 8 by this and in the middle margin shows *gotten riches* as a replacement for *virtuously*), *but you excelleth them all. Favor is deceitful* (ask any politician) *and beauty is vain* (or fleeting): *but the woman who feareth the Lord, she shall be praised. Give her of the fruit of her hands and let her own works praise her in the gates.* Here is a woman who has opportunity to receive praise for her works *in the gates*. At the time of this writing only men sat in the gates, and then, only elders, who had the knowledge and wisdom of experience to dispense to others. But we are told *Let her own works praise her in the gates.*

The Bible tells us in the New Testament book of Matthew 7: 16 *Ye shall know them by their fruits. Do men gather grapes of thorns or figs of thistles?* We read in the Old Testament book of Psalms 111: 10 *The fear of the Lord is the beginning of wisdom:* and in the Old Testament book of Isaiah 66: 2 *...but to this man* (or woman, since God is no respecter of persons), *will I look, even to him that is poor and of a contrite spirit, and trembleth at my words.* In other words, has things in the right perspective.

IN SUMMATION

In considering what is written here regarding the *Proverbs 31 Woman*, I think we can more easily see how these things can be more readily fulfilled by women of today as they don't have the same restrictions on them as did the women at the time of the writing of Proverbs 31. Still, even today's woman with all the modern technology available to her would be hard pressed to do all that this woman is said to do, Therefore, I think we can see that what the scripture is really talking about is something far surpassing a physical person, culture, or society. This is in essence describing the *Holy City*, in the New Testament book of Revelations 21:2 *coming down from God out of heaven, adorned as a bride for her husband.* This is the *Marriage of the Lamb and* the *Bride of Christ.* Truly a woman *fit for him as a helper* as God said in the Old Testament book of Genesis 2: 18 he would make for Adam.

Note: In my Bible referring to the above scripture, there is a number 9 by the words *meet for him.* In the middle margin it shows the Hebrew word meaning *as before him.* Think about that! A helper that was *before him.* Adam was created first, but Eve was taken *out of Adam.* So, essentially, they were both *one* in the beginning. But who or what was the help that was *before* him? That would be the *ONE* who created him, the same *ONE* that sends down the fitting help in Revelation 21: 2 and Genesis 2:18.

I mentioned in the beginning that I often wondered why there was no *Proverbs 31 Man.* Well, there is. It is the Christ and his example just as the *Proverbs 31 Woman* is the very essence of his bride-to-be. The bride comes from the Father in heaven. She is not physical just as the Father is not physical. New Testament book of John 4: 24 *God is a Spirit: and they that worship him must worship him in spirit and in truth.*

DAVID'S EXAMPLE

In the Old Testament book of Psalms 112: 1 *Praise ye the Lord. Blessed is the man that feareth the Lord, that delighteth greatly in his commandments.* David was such a man. Yes, he had feet of clay, but God called him *"a man after my own heart,"*

This is found in the Old Testament book of I Samuel 13: 14 where Saul is told the kingdom is being taken from him and given to another. *But now thy kingdom shall not continue: the Lord hath sought a man after his own heart, and the Lord hath commanded him to be captain over his people, because you hath not kept that which the Lord commanded you.* David replaced Saul as king over Israel. Seeing such an example as this, we need to consider before we start picking out one another's faults. We are told in the New Testament book of Matthew 5: 48 *Be ye therefore perfect, even as your Father which is in heaven is perfect.* That is-Be, present progressive, become-ye perfect. Always trying to become more like God, *our Father*, as Jesus calls Him in the *Lord's Prayer* and elsewhere.

Women need no longer fear to hear of the Proverbs 31 Woman. And we don't need to resent not having a Proverbs 31 man, or husband, or children. Nor do we need to diminish ourselves because we feel we do not measure up to the Proverbs 31 Woman. Life is always moving forward. God told Moses in the Old Testament book of Exodus 14: 15 *And the Lord said unto Moses. Wherefore criest thou unto me? Speak unto the children of Israel, that they go forward.* We can see that the woman of today has progressed in knowledge, understanding, and ability to more readily do the things mentioned in Proverbs 31. The physical, material, mental things. However, the goal is to incorporate body, mind, spirit, into the perfect spiritual helpmeet for the perfect man/husband represented by the *Holy City* and the *Marriage of the Lamb.*

This goes beyond the physical even as Jesus went beyond the physical in his works and said those who come after him will do even greater works than he did because he was going to his Father. New Testament book of John 14:12 *Verily, verily, I say unto you, He that believeth on me, the works that I do shall he do also; and greater works than these shall he do; because I go unto my Father.*

Thus, the 21st century woman goes beyond the Proverbs 31 woman, even as the 22nd century woman will surpass the 21st century, and on beyond that, never-ending.

WEALTH—POVERTY—
RIGHTEOUSNESS

I'm going to speak about the above, considering things I've read recently as well as what is written in the Bible regarding it.

I read recently in a book I own about the life of "Cat" Stevens, who gave up all his wealth and joined the Muslim religion because he thought they had the best discipline. (Most righteous?) He seemed to have it all. Yet he willingly gave it all up because he thought his wealthy lifestyle and all it entailed was why he was so unhappy and unfulfilled.

This got me thinking about wealth versus poverty regarding God, or Allah, or any other name you choose to use for the *Supreme Being*.

WEALTH AN EVIL?

People who live in poverty, especially those who do so not by choice, would not agree with "Cat". We have been told so often that it is the disparity between the "haves" and the "have-nots" that is the root cause of all the problems in the world. Often this scripture in the Bible is used to 'back up' this belief from a Christian or religious standpoint. I Timothy 6:10 *For the love of money is the root of all evil: which while some coveted after, they have erred from the faith, and pierced themselves through with many sorrows.*

It is the *love* of money, not the money itself that is *the* (could be rendered *a)* root of all evil. Why? Because the love of anything that comes before God is idolatry, which is what happens when the focus is primarily on anything physical—in this case, money.

Those who have it want to hold onto it at all costs and still want more, while those who don't have it resent those who do...all the while wanting to have it themselves.

THE EXAMPLE OF THE ISRAELITES

Israel continuously prayed to be delivered out of their bitter bondage to the Egyptians. Yet we find that, once they were delivered, at the first 'bump in the road', so to speak, they immediately wanted to return to Egypt. Old Testament book of Exodus 16: 2-3 *And the whole congregation of the children of Israel murmured against Moses and Aaron in the wilderness: and the children of Israel said unto them: Would to God we had died by the hand of the Lord in the land of Egypt, when we sat by the flesh pots, and when we did eat bread to the full; for you have brought us forth into this wilderness, to kill this whole assembly with hunger.*

(3) Wherefore the people did chide with Moses, and said, Give us water that we may drink. And Moses said unto them, Why chide you with me? Wherefore do you tempt the Lord? And the people thirsted there for water, and the people murmured against Moses, and said, Wherefore is this that thou hast brought us up out of Egypt, to kill us and our children and our cattle with thirst?

How quickly they forgot the miracles *God* performed to deliver them as they focused only on the physical events and the men, Moses and Aaron. This is the danger of putting your focus on anything, any person, any place, any object, that takes precedent over God. It can become your idol, which you are commanded not to have or make. Old Testament book of Exodus 20: 3-4 *Thou shalt have no other gods before me (2) Thou shalt not make unto thee any graven image, or any likeness of anything that is in heaven above, or that is in the earth beneath, or that is in the water under the earth.* The Israelites wanted out of slavery to the Egyptians but wanted to be like them as far as everything else went...the power and wealth, etc.

THE GOD OF MAMMON

We read in the New Testament book of Matthew 6:24 *No man can serve two masters, for either he will hate the one, and love the other; or else he will hold to the one and despise the other. Ye cannot serve God and mammon.* Mammon in this case being the god of wealth. This is shown by the commandment listed in the above paragraph. This is mentioned again in the New Testament book of Luke16:13 *No servant can serve two masters: for either he will hate the one, and love the other; or else he will hold to the one and despise the other.*

The Supreme Being does not say not to have other gods, only none that are before (or in place of) the One who is speaking. In the New Testament book of John10: 33-35 *The Jews answered him, saying, For a good work we stone thee not; but for blasphemy; and because that you, being a man, maketh yourself God. (34) Jesus answered them, Is it not written in your law, I said, ye are gods?* This is quoted from Psalm 82:6 in the Old Testament, *I have said, Ye are god; and all of you are children of the most High.* John 10:35 *If he called them gods, unto whom the word of God came, and the scripture cannot be broken,; (36) Say ye of him, whom the Father hath sanctified, and sent into the world, Thou blasphemest; because I said, I am the Son of God?*

GOD OWNS EVERYTHING

We find this in the Old Testament book of Haggai 2:8 *The silver is mine, and the gold is mine, saith the Lord of hosts.*

And in the Old Testament book of Ezekial 18:4 *Behold, all souls are mine, as the soul of the father, so also the soul of the son is mine: the soul that sinneth, it shall die.* We see from this that everything is God's, both physical and non-physical.

So, if the gold and silver are God's, and all souls are God's; this makes God the wealthiest of all. Therefore, how can we conclude that God thinks poor people are more righteous than wealthy people? Or that people of wealth are somehow more worthy than poor people because of their wealth?

The problem comes in because wealthy people tend to rely on their riches while poor people have none to rely on. However, not all wealthy people rely on their wealth. To name a few who relied on God instead of their wealth: Abraham, Isaac, Jacob and Job. Job was an example of a man who had it all and lost it all and still relied on God, and in the end, it was restored to him double.

SOLOMON'S PITFALL

Solomon, who asked for wisdom rather than riches, was given overflowing riches as well. To those who will say, "Yes, but look what happened to Solomon in the end" ... I remind you that it was not his wealth that brought about his downfall; but the way he *thought*. Once he began trying to appease his many wives, listening to them rather than his counselors and the counsel of God; he lost his wisdom. Solomon has asked for wisdom to lead the people. The Bible says in the Old Testament book of Proverbs 1:7 *The fear of the Lord is the beginning of knowledge: but fools despise wisdom and instruction*. My Bible has a 2 by the word *is*, and the marginal reference says *the principal part*. So, we can also read this as: *The fear of the Lord is the principal part of knowledge.*

Th following verses speak of listening to your parents and other wise counsel and not to follow those who seek gain by taking advantage of the innocent or through violence. Verse 19, *So are the ways of everyone that is greedy of gain: which takes away the life of the owner thereof.*

You don't have to literally take someone's life to do as the scripture says. You take away their life by stealing their identity and/or savings and livelihood. Do we have any of this going on today? But this is a two-edged sword, that also takes the life of the perpetrator. Same verse. Being greedy of gain takes away the life of the owner thereof. Because they have made gain their god in place of the Living God who owns everything, and their reward is to receive what they have done to another.

THE ANSWER

The Old Testament book of Proverbs also gives the answer to how we can understand *the fear of the Lord*. Proverbs 2:1-6 *My son, if thou wilt receive my words, and hide my commandment with thee; (2) so that thou incline thine ear to wisdom, and apply thine heart to understanding; (3) yes, if thou criest after knowledge, and liftest up thy voice after understanding: (4) if thou seekest her as silver, and searchest for her as for hid treasures; (5) Then shalt thou understand the fear of the Lord, and find the knowledge of God. (6) For the Lord giveth wisdom: out of his mouth cometh knowledge and understanding.* And in Proverbs 3:13-14 *Happy is the man that findeth wisdom, and the man that getteth, understanding. (14) For the merchandise of it is better than the merchandise of silver, and the gain thereof than fine gold.* This speaks of riches that are beyond the physical yet will also bring the physical riches as happened to Solomon. Solomon's wisdom spread through all the known world and is still spoken of today. And in the New Testament book of Matthew 6:33 *But seek ye first the kingdom of God, and his righteousness, and all these things shall be added unto you.*

THE "CATCH 22"

Jesus gives us a good analogy of the "Catch 22" situation found so often in human behavior and attitudes in the New Testament book of Luke 7: 31-35 And the Lord said, *whereunto then shall I liken the men of this generation? and to what are they like? (32) They are like unto children sitting in the marketplace, and calling one to another, and saying, We have piped unto you, and ye have not danced; we have mourned to you, and ye have not wept. (33) For John the Baptist came neither eating bread nor drinking wine; and ye say, He hath a devil. (34) The Son of man is come eating and drinking; and ye say, Behold a gluttonous man, and a winebibber, a friend of publicans and sinners. (35) But wisdom is justified of her children.* Never satisfied no matter how things are. They are either too "holy" or too "worldly", by *man's* standards. We can't seem to make a connection that there is a balance between the two. It is not an either/or, but a both/and.

THE LESSON OF THE MONARCHY

This was brought home to me one night while watching the documentary series *Monarchy*. The people were never satisfied and always wanted to impose, even by violent means, the way they thought things should be—especially regarding God and religion.

The series ended with the life of Oliver Cromwell, who was given the title "*King Killer*", because it was under his leadership the king was beheaded and the monarchy abolished. Yet, lo and behold! It was found *not* to have solved the problem and several years later the monarchy was reestablished.

This is much like the politics of this country (USA). The Republicans blame the Democrats, and the Democrats blame the Republicans. They continue to go back and forth, never seeming able to work together for the greater good of all. And our president is the closest thing to a monarch we have.

I am not knocking this country or any other. We all need to understand that the way of man is not in himself. Old Testament book of Jeremiah 10:23 *O Lord, I know that the way of man is not in himself: it is not in man that walketh to direct his steps.* Until we learn this lesson, we will continue to have those who seek riches because of greed and the power over others those riches can bring, causing wars and untold misery upon their fellow souls as a result of their greed regardless as to what form of government is in place.

Throughout history there have always been those who *think* they know a better way, and if they can just *impose* it on others then, the others will be happy despite themselves. Wrong! No one wants to be forced to do anything. They will always resist, even if only in their mind. But make no mistake...as soon as they have power to change this, they will!

BACK TO WEALTH VS POVERTY

Neither wealth, nor poverty, nor any other thing is *proof of favoritism* with God. In the New Testament book of Mark 10: 23-25, we read, *And Jesus looked round about, and saith unto his disciples, How hardly shall they that have riches enter into the kingdom of God. (24) And the disciples were astonished at his words. But Jesus answereth again, and saith unto them, Children, how hard is it for them that trust in riches to enter into the kingdom of God! (25) It is easier for a camel to go through the eye of a needle, than for a rich man to enter into the kingdom of God.*

The disciples were astonished and began to wonder how anyone could be saved as they had given up all to follow Christ, verses 26-31. Their answer was given in verse 27: *And Jesus looking upon them saith, With men it is impossible, but not with God: for with God all things are possible.*

This took place right after Jesus had told a wealthy man to sell all he had and give to the poor and take up his cross and follow him. Mark 10: 17-22. Was this because Jesus was against riches? Not at all. He knew the man was trusting in his wealth. Verse 22 *And he was sad at that saying and went away grieved: for he had great possessions.*

In the New Testament book of Mark 14:1-7, we have the case of the woman who brought an alabaster box of ointment of spikenard (a very expensive ointment) and broke the box and poured it on the head of Jesus. *(4) And there were some that had indignation within themselves, and said, Why was this waste of the ointment made? (5) For it might have been sold for more than three hundred pence, and have been given to the poor. And they murmured against her. (6) And Jesus said, Let her alone; why trouble ye her? She hath wrought a good work on me. (7) For ye hath the poor with you always, and whensoever ye will ye may do them good: but me ye have not always.*

Here Jesus showed them they can always do something to help the poor. They did not need a special occasion like using the expensive spikenard ointment. Perhaps we should ask ourselves if we can do more to help the poor or those less fortunate than ourselves, or do we wait for a special occasion to do something.

All things and all people belong to God. Both the rich and the poor. We are shown in the parable of *The Good Samaritan* found in the New Testament book of Luke 10: 30-37, that everyone is our neighbor whom we are to love as we do ourselves. In the New Testament book of Matthew 22; 36-40. Rich, poor, Israelite, non-Israelite...everyone! God is no respecter of persons. New Testament book of Acts 10:34 *Then Peter opened his mouth, and said, Of a truth I perceive that God is no respecter of persons: (35) but in every nation he that feareth him, and worketh righteousness, is accepted with him.*

This covers all people and situations. The poor don't need to condemn the rich and the rich don't need to look down on the poor. All are God's no matter their status. Rather than claiming one or the other shows God's preference for righteousness; why not work together to lift each other up to the kind of life that will depict God's kingdom on Earth?

JUDGE NOT

Recently I was thinking on the injunction *judge not*. I know from personal experience with religion in the past, having spent some forty years with one group, that most feel they *need* to judge whether a thing, person, or action is "right" or "wrong", according to their belief system and that of their group, and therefore, worthy of "praise" or "condemnation".

There is the tendency to think that now that they have been baptized and are following the rules and laws of whatever group they relate to; they are therefore free from sin and in order to stay that way they must be on the alert to what others are doing that may affect them negatively. They feel they can judge whether something is "good" or "bad" since they have been cleansed and are no longer *spotted* by the world. I say this because *I* formerly believed the same way.

WHAT THE BIBLE SAYS ABOUT THIS

Let's look at what the Bible says about this since that is where the injunction comes from. We read in the New Testament book of Matthew 7:1 *Judge not, that ye be not judged...*It then goes on to show *why* you should not judge and shows that the judgment it is here speaking of carries within it a rendering of punishment and/or condemnation. Continuing: *For with what judgment ye judge, ye shall be judged: and with what measure ye mete, it shall be measured to you again.*

There is a saying familiar to most of us: *what goes around, comes around*. This scripture is saying the same thing.

Continuing: verses 3-5 *And why beholdest thou the mote that is in thy brother's eye, but considerest not the beam that is in thine own eye? (4) or wilt thou say to thy brother, Let me pull out the mote out of thine eye; and behold, a beam is in thine own eye? (5) Thou hypocrite, first cast out the beam out of thine own eye; and then shalt thou see clearly to cast out the mote out of thy brother's eye.*

Could it be that we are so intent on what another is doing or not doing, that we forget to examine our own reason for judging our brother? Are we worthy to do it?

I am sure those who think they must judge are really thinking they *discern a difference*. Yet even that is to put something between and leads right back to a judgment instead of seeing something as a *preference*. You may or may not prefer what another says or does, but you need not judge them as being "wrong" in it. For if you consider them "wrong", it usually implies a need for correction or punishment (a judgment), rather than just something they chose that you would not choose.

We read this in the New Testament book of Romans 14:4 *Who art thou that judgest another man's servant? To his own master he standeth or falleth. Yea, he shall be holden up: for God is able to make him stand.*

DO UNTO OTHERS

Reminding us that with what measure we mete, it will be measured to us again is another way of stating the *Golden Rule* found in the New Testament book of Matthew 7:12 Therefore *all things whatsoever ye would that men should do to you, do ye even so to them: for this is the law and the prophets.* (The fulfillment of all that is written in the law and the prophets.)

Every law, every rule, every commandment given to the people of Israel, including the laws of health, as well as the holy days and tithes, were given to teach them how to love God and their neighbor as themselves.

In Matthew 22:36 Jesus is asked which is the great commandment of the law. Jesus answered in 37-39 *Thou shalt love the Lord thy God with all thy heart, with all your soul, and with all your mind. (38) This is the first and great commandment. (39) And the second is like unto it, Thou shalt love thy neighbor as thyself. (40) On these two hang all the law and the prophets.* Once again, we find everything in the law and the prophets is fulfilled in these two commandments.

And for those who are not sure who is their neighbor whom they are to love as themselves, we find the answer in the Parable of the Good Samaritan found in the New Testament book of Luke 10: 29-37. <u>Everyone</u> is your neighbor. We are to love everyone as we love God and as we love ourselves. This leaves no room for superior/inferior, or any other idea used to separate between people and to judge others that continues to this day to cause division and mistrust and hatred and wars.

So, follow the injunction and *Judge Not!*

PATRIOTISM

This is a subject almost everyone can relate to. Let me begin by assuring you that I am not going to be knocking *Patriotism,* although I realize it may seem that way to some who read this. Read on anyway before you come to any conclusion to see if you are correct in your perception.

Patriotism relates to progenitor, place of birth, parents, beginnings, to *father,* especially. If you are a patriot, it shows you are loyal to the father, or country, or founding group you are a part of. We are all aware there are many countries on this planet we all share, and many patriots to whatever is that country's cause.

In the United States of America, our national anthem has the words: *home of the brave, land of the free.* We know of Germany's *"Fatherland",* as well as Russia's *"Mother Russia".* We read, hear, or use these words without giving them much thought. And everyone knows how moving are marches and alma mater music used at football games and other sports events. They do a great job of raising our emotions to fever pitch, even if we are not personally involved with or part of the group being promoted at the time. I know that *I* am personally moved by them.

Then there are the uniforms. They also influence us, both positive and negative, depending on the circumstances. So, it is not surprising that the two of them are used together to create a particular desired response from those on both sides of the equation, pro and con.

A RECENT EXAMPLE

Some time ago, I had occasion to attend a concert with a friend of mine, during which the band leader took time to say some things to "show support for our troops", along with some music guaranteed to win the hearts of the listeners and have them "get on the bandwagon" with him in this regard.

As I observed all this, I had a thought that is culminating in this writing. The thought was this: I want to write something about this and how, what we really need is a *Universal Patriotism* and *Anthem*.

I know there will be those who will immediately think I am using different words for the old concept of *world dominion*, only subtly implying that the United States of America should be the leader of such because, after all, I am an American citizen and therefore a patriot, right? If not, perhaps I think another country is better suited for the job?

I am an American citizen and happen to think it is the best country to live in at the time of this writing because of all the freedom found here. But I also am not blind to the inequities found here. If there were not any there would be no need for change of any kind. Change is needed in every country on this planet.

HOME OF THE BRAVE, LAND OF THE FREE

Referring to the above, let us see if there are any brave enough to consider what I am saying throughout this writing without precluding it as an attack. Brave enough to apply it in their own lives if, after considering it, they find it worth a try. Because they *do* have the freedom to do just that here in this "*Land of the Free*". It is for this reason I consider everyday a *Day of Thanksgiving*, not just once a year.

Permit me a moment here to clarify what I just said. As I read over it, I realized it sounds patriotic, especially to the United States of America. That's fine, as far as it goes. However, a *Universal* Patriotism would include everyone in—well, the Universe! By this alone, it would supersede all countries on this planet as well as anywhere else countries may be found.

A HIGHER POWER

Those who believe in a *Higher Power,* by whatever name, would be willing to jump on the bandwagon, so to speak, if *their Higher Power* were to be the one awarded this "*Universal Patriotism*". This is no different from the attitudes that already exist behind nationalism of every kind.

To even choose one means that those who already honor that *One* are right, and the rest are wrong. Right? Wrong! To even choose in such a manner would be to deny the *Greatest Power* of all and would continue the one-upmanship going on for millennia between people, communities, nations. This power I speak of is the ALL-THAT-IS, the SOURCE ENERGY that creates everything and cannot be limited to one people, place, time or space.

CHRISTIAN IDEALS

To those who will say I am using the *Christian Bible and God* for my ideal expressed in this writing, I say, "You are right, but only to a point." The God of which I speak is the one calling itself "I AM". The one who spoke with Moses at the burning bush in Exodus 3 in the Old Testament. This *I AM* speaks to us through the Apostle Peter in the New Testament book of Acts 10: 34-45 *Then Peter opened his mouth, and said, of a truth I perceive that God is no respecter of persons; but in every nation, he that feareth him, and worketh righteousness, is accepted with him.* We find in the New Testament book of James 2:9 *But if ye have respect to persons, ye commit sin, and are convinced (convicted), of the law as transgressors.* Do we have any respect of persons going on today, even among Christians?

PURPOSE OF THE LAW

Every law, sacrifice, offering, holy day, commandment, tithe, et al, were given to try to teach the physical nation a spiritual principle: how to love God and their neighbor as themselves. The two great commandments listed in Matthew 22: 36-40 (New Testament). The fledgling nation of Israel was to be the model for all the surrounding nations.

In the New Testament book of Matthew 7: 12, we find the text that has come to be known as *The Golden Rule. Therefore all things whatsoever ye would that men should do to you, do ye even so to them: for this is the law and the prophets.*(This is the fulfilling of the purpose of the law and the prophets.) And we find in Luke 10: 25-37, the parable of the *Good Samaritan*, that <u>everyone</u> *is our neighbor*. By treating others as you want them to treat you, there can be <u>no respect of persons</u>.

ALL SOULS BELONG TO GOD

We are told through the prophet Ezekial in the Old Testament book of Ezekial 18:4 *Behold all souls are mine; as the soul of the father, so also the soul of the son is mine...*and we have already been shown that God is no respecter of persons and that we should treat others the way we want to be treated. Considering all this, doesn't it behoove us...all of us...to rethink this concept of *Patriotism*?

NO SPECIAL TREATMENT

If we are all God's, and the Great I AM says that we are, this One who is no respecter of persons; doesn't it seem logical that we should have a *Universal Patriotism* and *Anthem*? Don't you think you would be moved by such an anthem that included equally, everyone, everywhere, in all times, places, and spaces?

THINK ABOUT IT!

THE POWER OF BELIEF
TO FREE OR IMPRISON

I've been giving thought to several beliefs addressed in the Bible that not only affected the people in those times we refer to as *Bible Times* but continue to impact our lives today. One such belief is:

AGEISM: We tend to hold the belief that as people age, they become less useful and, in fact, become a hinderance and burden on society. Under Hitler's regime in Germany in the late 1930's - 1940's, this was carried to an extreme. Starting with their own people they did away with the old and infirm and those who were in some way *imperfect,* moving on to those of other races who were considered less than perfect, while seeking to build a *superior race* of Aryans. Our hospitals and nursing homes are filled with people who suffer from this belief of ageism, (or were put there by others who hold the belief). They believe it and they reap the harvest of their belief. Am I saying you will not age, grow old and die? Not at all. What I *am* saying is that it doesn't have to be the way we've been taught and passed down for generations.

EXAMPLE OF SARAH AND ABRAHAM

In the Bible we have the account of Sarah and Abraham who had a child in their old age. Sarah was 90 and Abraham was 100. This was after her *time of women* had passed. In other words, she was past menopause, and Abraham was old also. The Bible asks the question found in the Old Testament book of Genesis 18: 14 *Is anything too hard for the Lord? At the time appointed I will return unto thee, according to the time of life, and Sarah shall have a son.* God was going to return to them the ability to procreate and produce a son as promised. Sarah herself suffered from age belief, which is why she laughed when she heard they would have a child. Genesis 18: 11-12 *Now Abraham and Sarah were old and well stricken in age; and it ceased to be with Sarah after the manner of women. (12) Therefore Sarah laughed within herself, saying, After I am waxed old shall I have pleasure, my lord being old also?* God did not let her unbelief keep him from fulfilling the promise made to Abraham. In fact, after the death of Sarah at age 127, Abraham married again and produced six more sons. Since he was 10 years older than Sarah, this meant that he went on at age 137 to produce more children. Hardly fits in with today's societal beliefs, does it?

BARREN: Another belief is that if a person is barren or infertile, they are doomed as far as having children are concerned. The only option left to them is to adopt or be left childless.

However, we have an example in the Old Testament book of I Samuel 1: 1-28. We find the account of Hannah, who was barren but petitioned the Lord for a son, promising to give him to the Lord's service for all his life.

Her petition was granted, and her son was the prophet Samuel whom God called at an early age to minister to him. (Samuel was another son of promise. This time a woman's promise to God.) Hannah's belief in God's ability to perform what she asked brought her the answer to her petition, as it is written in the New Testament book of Matthew 9: 29 *Then touched he their eyes, saying, According to your faith be it done unto you.*

TWO POWERFUL EXAMPLES

POSITIVE: We find the example of Elijah mentioned in the New Testament book of James 5: 17 *Elias was a man subject to like passions as we are, and he prayed earnestly that it might not rain: and it rained not on the earth by the space of three years and six months. (18) And he prayed again, and the heaven gave rain, and the earth brought forth her fruit.* A man of like passions. Just like us. What set him apart was his powerful belief that he would receive from God what he asked. This is a positive example, and shows God is no respecter of persons. New Testament book of Ephesians 6: 9 *And ye masters, do the same things unto them, forbearing threatening: knowing that your Master also is in heaven; neither is there any respect of persons with him.* Read also the account of the contest between Elijah and the priests of Baal in I Kings 18.

NEGATIVE: In the Old Testament book of Job, we find the account of Job's powerful belief in the negative bringing exactly that to him. Job 3: 25 *For the thing which I greatly feared is come upon me, and that which I was afraid of is come unto me.* Job had a strong focus of belief that he would lose his children and he offered sacrifices continually on their behalf to try to stave off the inevitable. Job was imprisoned by the power of his faith in the negative happening.

Today we hear much about the *Law of Attraction.* I have just given two examples of this, showing it works both ways: positive and/or negative. Think about this when you are asking for something. What is your purpose for wanting what you are asking for? Understand that you have more power than you ever thought possible. Then act from positive faith and belief.

NEW TESTAMENT EXAMPLES

In the New Testament we find a testament to unbelief when it is written that he (Jesus), could not there do many mighty works *because of their unbelief.* Matthew 13: 58. We find out why in verse 57. *And they were offended in him. But Jesus said unto them. A prophet is not without honor, save in his own country, and in his own house.* They suffered from that old belief that says, *'You can't be anybody because I know you.'*

If only people really understood what they were saying about themselves by this belief. Therefore, people who came to Jesus for healing were told it was done unto them according to their faith. Some were even asked, *Believest thou I am able to do this?* They had to believe, or the healing would not take place.

An example of weak faith or doubt is found in the account of Peter being imprisoned after the death of James, the brother of John. The people prayed for Peter and an angel came and freed him from prison. But when Peter came to the place where they were, and a damsel went to tell them Peter stood at the door...*they didn't believe her!* New Testament book of Acts 12: 1-16. This is a great example of our weak faith which leads to the next reason why we don't get as many miracles in our lives as we'd like to receive.

A BELIEF IN UNWORTHINESS

I think we can trace this back all the way to the Garden of Eden, the story of Adam and Eve, and so-called *original sin*. We read in the Old Testament book of Genesis the story of Adam and Eve in the Garden of Eden, or Paradise, as it is sometimes called because everything was perfect for them there until they ate of the fruit of the *tree of knowledge of good and evil* against God's command and were driven out and kept away by powerful beings with flaming swords. Genesis, chapter 3.

This false belief (unworthiness) has been handed down from generation to generation, continually perpetuating misery, unhappiness and fear. Fear of a God who claims to be *Love*, and *Unconditional* Love, at that.

Even the belief in *Reincarnation,* as it is commonly accepted, is predicated on the idea of returning to another physical life in order to atone for sins and misdeeds in the previous life (or lives), as a sort of punishment. Give this some thought and you will see that you would <u>never</u> become worthy! Besides trying to make up for past deeds you would be creating new ones in the present life to be dealt with in yet another life... never ending.

Does this sound like a requirement of a God of unconditional love? In fact, if there are *any* conditions at all, then God's love is *not unconditional.* We read in the Old Testament book of Jeremian 31: 3 *The Lord hath appeared of old unto me, saying, Yea, I have loved thee with an everlasting love: therefore with lovingkindness have I drawn thee.* An everlasting love does not have conditions. This includes a belief in laws that need to be obeyed in order not to offend God, causing you to lose favor and maybe your place in heaven. My mind cannot compute this; a God who loves everlastingly and unconditionally; but will send you to an ever-burning hell if you make him mad enough. Doesn't this sound more like the gods of the nations that were around Israel? Their idea of a greater power, but one so much like them that they, in fact, created their god in their own image. Have we fallen prey to the same error?

EVERYTHING OLD IS NEW AGAIN

The saying above is from a movie starring Julie Andrews in which she sings about it being 1922, *modern times.*

It is the same today: parents using the example of their children doing something that displeases them causing them to be out of favor with their parents and to feel unworthy of their parents' love because of their words or actions. Parents use this to keep their children in line. Friends and lovers use this to manipulate each other in order to get what they want. We have fostered off on God our behavior toward others as if God said it first and that's why we do it. In doing so we have made God in our own image instead of us being made in the image of God. Nowhere do you find God telling you to manipulate others. Rather, you are told to love others as yourself. New Testament book of Matthew 22: 39 *And the second is like unto it, Thou shalt love thy neighbor as thyself.* You need only to ask yourself if you want your neighbor to treat you as you may have been treating him to find your answer as to whether you are living by the old or the new way.

Belief is very powerful! No one wants to think they are "wrong" in their beliefs. No one wants to think that what their parents, teachers, etc., taught them was "wrong". That someone could hate you and try to destroy you if you try to get them to see things in a different way than they have seen them for generations should not be surprising. Christ is a perfect example of this. His death was fostered by those of the highest offices in the Jewish religion who feared him, and that his teachings might take away their authority and the honor they received from the people. It was *professional jealousy!*

PEOPLE BELIEVE WHAT THEY KNOW IS NOT TRUE

It seems strange to say that people believe in something that they know is not true, but you need look no further than the custom and culture of

Christmas, which gets bigger each year it seems. Those who have looked more than superficially into the *Christian religion* know where most of these *holidays* come from. They were *pagan* festivals given a new name to make them palpable to the population they were trying to make proselytes of for the Christian Church. You can look this up for yourself in church history if you are interested. It's much easier to do something if everyone else is doing it too. Thus, the "new" old holidays.

Am I saying you should stop keeping all the holidays you keep at present because of their mostly pagan origins? Not at all.

In fact, I have found it interesting, in watching many of the Christmas movies on television, how people show their longing for a greater power to "grant wishes" and "perform miracles". They give this "power" to *Santa Claus* and tell everyone to remember *Anything is possible at Christmas!* In other words, *believe, have faith.* And the best part of all...Santa doesn't punish, even though it's said he brings toys for all the *good* little boys and girls. So, people want someone who will grant them what they wish for, provide miracles when needed (and after they've exhausted all other means), and be kind and generous and understanding. But this person (*Santa Claus*), only comes once a year even though he supposedly sees you and knows if you've been naughty or nice.

If this suits you and makes you happy (even though little kids are not happy when they find out "Santa" isn't real), keep doing it. Just don't pretend that this is God's doings. God's miracles are every day—not once a year. People choosing this over the true God reminds me of what the people told Moses in the Old Testament book of Exodus 20: 18-19 *And all the people saw the thunderings, and the lightnings, and the noise of the trumpet, and the mountain smoking: and when the people saw it, they removed, and stood afar off. (19) And they said unto Moses, Speak thou with us, and we will hear: but let not God speak with us, lest we die.*

Why would they think they would die if God spoke with them? Because they *knew in their belief of unworthiness that they* could not stand before the power of God. Yet Moses was also a man, albeit one who believed God and to whom God said he knew face to face. Old Testament book of Deuteronomy 34: 10 *And there arose not a prophet since in Israel like unto Moses, whom the Lord knew face to face.* And in the New Testament book of I Corinthians 13: 12 *For now we see through a glass darkly, but then face to face; now I know in part; but then shall I know even as also I am known.*

The time is coming when all will know and be known. Then there will be no need for anyone to be imprisoned by their beliefs because the *truth shall make you free.* New Testament book of John 8: 32 *And ye shall know the truth, and the truth shall make you free.*

ONLY BELIEVE

This is in reference to something I've been learning about recently pertaining to believing versus doing.

I spoke with a friend recently who was experiencing the same uncertainty I was regarding deciding about something. I did not tell my friend at the time that I was experiencing the same thing, albeit on a different subject. My desire was to listen to her and perhaps learn from the conversation myself while trying to encourage her. I had found some time ago that in every interaction like this there is usually something for me to learn from it. This time was no different.

We both believed we are cared for by God, or Source, or whatever name you choose to use in reference to the great power that creates worlds. And we both had experiences in the past that proved to us the validity of our belief.

Still, we found ourselves in a bit of a quandary at this time because we couldn't seem to make up our minds to do something or not. It's not that we were thinking of doing something wrong or hurtful to another...quite the opposite. What we were thinking of doing had the potential of being helpful to others as well as ourselves. So, why the conundrum?

JUST DECIDE

I think we are all familiar with the Nike saying, "*Just do it*!" I finally told my friend at one point, (really giving myself the same advice), "You know what you need to do?" "What?" she asked. "You need to make a decision." I told her. "Just decide, and if, after having done that and following through you find it was not as good a choice as you thought—then, make another decision and change that."

I realized later that was exactly what *I* needed to do regarding my waffling on my own decision making. Just decide! Then you and the Universe have something to work with. The Bible tells us in the New Testament book of James1:8 *a double minded man is unstable in all his ways.* And he is. Swinging first one way and then the other. Unable to be relied on because of indecision. We are told in the Bible if we are that way, James 1:7 *Let not that man think he receives anything of the Lord.* How can he? The Lord doesn't know what he wants because he keeps changing it!

We are told in the New Testament book of Matthew 13:58 *And he did not many mighty works there because of their unbelief.* Doubt is unbelief and resistance. It was not that they kept Christ from his ability. Rather, they kept themselves from receiving because of their unbelief.

If we doubt ourselves as well as God, we are resisting the good that can come to us. One way we doubt ourselves and God is through belief in *unworthiness.* God cannot give you what you want and may even ask for— if you believe you don't deserve it. It's the same as not asking anyway. You have negated it before it even gets started. Then, when you don't receive what you ask for, that "little voice" in your head says, *"See! I told you so!"* This is the fruit of the *Catch-22* of double minded thinking: confusion, instability, unhappiness and unwanted things in our lives.

TO BE OR TO DO—THAT IS THE QUESTION

I realized later, after the conversation with my friend, that we were doing what people all over the world tend to do regardless of their religious affiliation. We were thinking there was something we needed to do to either please God by carrying out our part, or maybe it was what God would want us to do, or perhaps how God would answer our petition.

In times past people have followed rituals, etc., that they were instructed to follow for them to receive their request. It occurs to me that this is possibly why God gave Israel certain instructions—having to do something in order to receive what was promised. (*Trying to make themselves worthy to receive by whatever it was they would do.*)

However, following rituals and such will never give people the *faith* or *belief* they truly need in order to accomplish great things in their lives because they *are doing* something instead. In the New Testament book of Hebrews 9:12 *Neither by the blood of goats and calves, but by his own blood he entered in once into the holy place, having obtained eternal redemption for us.* The physical sacrifices took a lot of *doing* on all parts.

This was the conundrum of my friend and myself. Were we to do something ourselves, or believe God meant it when he said he would care for us and provide all our needs?

A NEW WAY OF DOING

The New Testament of the Bible is the account of the birth, life, works, death, and resurrection of the man called Jesus Christ and of his followers. There are some that believe that with the advent of Christ on the scene the Old Testament no longer has relevancy for us. And there are those who believe the opposite is true: all the old laws, rituals, etc., are still in effect and that, in fact; Christ still has not come.

In this modern age I don't think those of the old persuasion still kill lambs or goats or bulls, as part of their belief (at least here in the USA). But they may look around them and feel they are right to continue the way they have believed for generations.

I have come to see that whatever your accepted belief, you will seek and find *evidence* to support and backup said belief. This holds true regardless as to whether others believe the same way or not. Those who do not believe will also seek and find *evidence* to support and back up their unbelief. Why? How can this be?

Each one believes he is "right", and the other is "wrong", because of their *evidence*. What does the Bible say about this? Old Testament book of Proverbs 21:2 *Every way of a man is right in his own eyes; but the Lord ponders the heart.* God is interested in the intention, not the outward show. We are also told to *Seek and ye shall find.* This sums up for us the *why* answer to the above question. If you truly seek something you *will* find an answer as God is no respecter of persons. But—and this is a big "but"— *why are you seeking it?* Do you truly want to understand, or do you want to "prove" yourself *right* and the other *wrong?*

This writing has to do with the belief that Jesus called Christ did in fact come and by many works showed a way that goes beyond the old to a deeper understanding of how to live the fulfillment of what the old rituals, laws, offerings, etc., portrayed.

As such, I will continue what Jesus said about this subject of *belief.* In the New Testament book of Luke 8:50 *Fear not: believe only, and she shall be made whole.* I realized I needed to be like the man in the Bible who said to Jesus in the New Testament book of Mark 9:24 *And straightway the father of the child cried out, and said with tears, Lord, I believe; help thou mine unbelief.* (In areas where I am weak in faith or belief, help me to be strong.)

Those who came to him for healing believed he could do it or they would not have been healed. They were not told to do any certain thing but believe. Christ said in Mark 9:23 *And Jesus said unto him, if you canst believe, all things are possible to him that believeth.* He did not say, providing they do certain things or make certain sacrifices.

OLD TESTAMENT EXAMPLE OF SARAH AND ABRAHAM

Referring to the example in the Old Testament of Sarah and Abraham: God told them they would have a child, Genesis 18:10 *And he said, I will certainly return unto you according to the time of life; and, lo, Sarah thy wife shall have a son. And Sarah heard it in the tent door which was behind him.* Now they were both old and Sarah was past the time of women (menopause). The next verses show that Sarah laughed because she did not believe but denied it when she was called out on it because she was afraid. Abraham did believe. They were told in verse 14 *Is anything too hard for the Lord? At the time appointed I will return unto thee, according to the time of life, and Sarah shall have a son.*

When time went by without a son forthcoming, they began to think of other ways God may use to fulfill the promise—at least, Sarah did. When she offered her young handmaiden to her husband to raise up a child by that means and he accepted, you must wonder if Abraham too, was starting to think God may use it as a means of fulfilling the promise. (Forgetting that God specifically said *Sarah* would have a son.)

A reading of what followed in the Bible will show that it didn't work out like they thought. In fact, it backfired on them. However, God still gave them a son together as promised. Genesis 21: 1-3 *And the Lord visited Sarah as he had said, and the Lord did unto Sarah as he had spoken. (2) For Sarah conceived, and bare Abraham a son in his old age, at the time of which God had spoken to him.* God was not limited by their age or anything else. God is still not limited today by age or anything else.

In the New Testament book of Luke, we are told 21:19 In *your patience possess ye your soul.* Patience is a virtue most of us seem to be lacking in, which leads us to try to figure out how we think God may work something out for us since we are told "ask and you shall receive". Instinctively we know better, but we still tend to do it anyway (as Sarah and Abraham did), when an answer isn't immediately forthcoming.

WHAT ABOUT WORKS?

If we are to only believe, what about works? Where do they come in—or do they?

The apostle Paul lamented in The New Testament book of Romans 7: 19-24 *For the good that I would, I do not: but the evil that I would not, that I do. (20) Now if I do that I would not, it is no more I that doeth it, but sin that dwelleth in me. (21) I find then a law, that when I would do good, evil is present with me. (22) For I delight in the law of God after the inward man: (23) but I see another law in my members, warring against the law of my mind, and bringing me into captivity to the law of sin which is in my members. (24) O wretched man that I am! Who shall deliver me from the body of this death? (25) I thank God through Jesus Christ our Lord. So then with the mind I myself serve the law of God; but with the flesh the law of sin.*

Old habits die hard. We have been programmed from birth to believe we are either unworthy to receive or there are certain things we must do first to show God our faith and belief, (our goodness and worthiness to receive), by whatever rituals, sacrifices, offerings, etc., we are told to do in order to gain God's acceptance. Jesus said, *only believe.* Since he was the physical sacrifice that ended the need for physical sacrifices, the only sacrifice we need to offer is *our belief.*

Therefore, we are told to come *boldly* before the throne of grace. New Testament book of Hebrews 4: 16 *Let us therefore come boldly unto the throne of grace, that we may obtain mercy, and find grace to help in time of need.* There is no longer any need for rituals or sacrifices: only a belief that God will perform what He says He will...period.

We are told it is done unto you according to your faith. New Testament book of Matthew 9: 29 *Then touched he their eyes saying, According to your faith be it done unto you.* Faith is a belief, and a belief is a thought you keep thinking. If you continue thinking this thought that becomes a belief it will become a *knowing.* Then, no action on our part is needed. Belief is the most powerful thing I know of.

We read in the New Testament book of Hebrews11: 6 *For without faith it is impossible to please him: for he that cometh to God must believe that he is, and that he is a rewarder of them that diligently seek him.* In the Old Testament book of Job 3: 25, we read Job's words *That which I greatly feared has come upon me.* It was Job's belief that what happened to him *would* happen, and he tried to ward it off by continually sacrificing, especially on behalf of his children. His belief that it would happen overrode his sacrifices and offerings. Could it be that Job also suffered from a belief in unworthiness, at least where his children were concerned, causing him to lose all he had despite his own righteousness? We just read above *according to your faith (belief), be it done unto you.* Job had to learn you cannot be righteous for anyone else.

We find in the New Testament book of Ephesians 2: 7-9 *That in the ages to come he might shew the exceeding riches of his grace in his kindness toward us through Christ Jesus (8) For by grace are you saved through faith; and that not of yourselves: it is the gift of God: (9) Not of works, lest any man should boast.* All the works one could possibly do cannot save you. But if you believe, you will be producing works that demonstrate your belief, as we read in the New Testament book of James 2: 17-20 *Even so faith, if it hath not works, is dead, being alone. (18) Yea, a man may say, Thou hast faith, and I have works: shew me thy faith without thy works, and I will shew thee my faith by my works. (19) Thou believest there is one God; thou doest well: the devils also believe, and tremble. (20) But wilt thou know, O vain man, that faith without works is dead?*

THE CONCLUSION

I started this writing telling of the confusion being experienced by a friend of mine and myself. I finally realized what was causing the confusion was that what we were contemplating doing *we really did not want to do*, just as I feel certain that Sarah did not really want her husband to go unto another woman in order to produce an heir. But in our ignorance and lack of understanding, we, like Sarah, were trying to figure out *how* God would do his work.

God tells us in the New Testament book of I Corinthians 2: 9 *Eye hath not seen, nor ear heard, neither hath entered into the heart of man, the things which God hath prepared for those who love him.*

We need to stop trying to come up with ways for God to provide for us and *Only Believe* as Jesus said. God will do the rest as promised.

CASTING THE NET

While watching the TV series *AD the Bible Continues* recently, the scene after the crucifixion of Jesus where he tells his disciples to cast their nets on the opposite side of the boat caught my attention as never before.

FOLLOWING THE NORM

After the death of Jesus, the disciples felt it was all over so, Peter said to the others, I go a fishing. New Testament book of John 21: 3 *Simon Peter saith unto them, I go a fishing. They say unto him, We also go with thee. They went forth, and entered into a ship immediately: and that night they caught nothing. (4) But when the morning was now come, Jesus stood on the shore: But the disciples knew not that it was Jesus.* Verses 5-8 give the account of Jesus telling them to cast their net on the other side of the ship and they did so, getting a haul of 153 great fish, and without breaking the net.

We find this account also in the New Testament book of Luke 5: 1-10, but it varies in that this is where Jesus tells them he will make them fishers of men. After the miracle of the catch, they left all and followed him. Before that, however, they followed the 'norm', which was the belief that death was the end.

FROM ORDINARY TO EXTRAORDINARY

I've read this account many times and seen it portrayed in movies, however, this time it was different for me. I started thinking about it in a way I never had before. A way of applying it to my own life. The same can apply to others as well.

How often do we think that what we do in life, especially in our jobs, has no bearing on the spiritual aspect of our lives? How many times have we perhaps wished for a life that made a difference like the apostles, but simply thought that we were not spiritual enough? That would be for the preachers and other "men of the cloth", we would usually think.

But these were ordinary men, fishermen, who were doing the job they were used to doing and had gone back to after the death of Jesus. Knowing all about fishing as I'm sure they felt they did, I imagine they had to wonder a bit at being told to cast their nets on the other side of the ship. After all, water was everywhere around the ship, and fish would be in the water available for them to catch.

Nevertheless, they showed openness of mind in casting their net on the other side of the ship. In the account written in John, we find the net did not break, but in the account of Luke, the catch was so great help was called for and the abundant catch was then brought to shore.

This could even be two accounts: the one showing Jesus calling Peter out to be the leader he had already shown himself to be and the other showing the need for teamwork to get the job done.

A PERSONAL LESSON

I started thinking about the lesson here. If they could catch such an abundance of fish simply by casting their net on the *right side of the boat*, would it not behoove me to inquire where to cast my net in order that my 'catch' be so richly abundant? They didn't discount advice from someone simply because they were fishermen and therefore, knowledgeable and maybe even "experts" on fishing. They were open to outside information and like the Bereans mentioned in the New Testament book of Acts 17: 11, *who searched the scriptures daily whether these things were so...*they cast their net on the other side to see if what they had been told had merit or not.

We have many decisions to make in our lives, many are seemingly mundane. Yet, if we were instructed where to cast our net (decisions), whether by spoken word, written word, or inspiration, we are sure to receive much more abundantly than if we simply do as we always have (the 'norm'), or as mankind always has.

LIFE MORE ABUNDANT

Jesus says in the New Testament book of John 10: 10, last part, *I am come that they may have life, and that they may have it more abundantly.*

We take so much for granted and move through our lives as in a dream, or, as if most of it doesn't matter because it's ordinary, everyday stuff that we do 'marking time' until something special or wonderful and exciting happens, or that we consider to be such.

What would my life be like, I wondered, if I should begin thinking about, and asking, *where to cast my net?* No one knows better than our *Source*, the answer to that whether it be called *God*, or *Allah*, or by any other name.

The Chinese have a saying: *No one steps in the same river twice.* Think about this and you will see the validity of it. The same should apply to where we cast our nets each day.

Each day is a new beginning, so why not see if we can increase our 'catch' (live our lives more abundantly), by seeking guidance on where to cast our nets?

By seeking help in making the decisions we make each day, we not only can increase our 'catch', but our daily lives will be much more open to exciting moments, rather than just *mundane tasks.* Even those tasks can take on a new life of their own as they are viewed with gratitude rather than as drudgery.

SIGNS

Many are content to let others tell them what to do and when to do it and with whom. We believe prayer is communicating with God, at least, we say that we do. But do we ever listen or is it strictly a one-way communication of us asking God for what we want. Do we even expect an answer, or is it just something we do, and hope things will turn out as we want?

I know there are those who will watch for a *sign* to judge what actions they should take (if any). I am not condemning "signs". After all, God put his rainbow in the sky as a *sign* that the earth would never again be destroyed by a flood. Others had signs throughout the Old Testament and the New. But Jesus told Herod, *a wicked and adulterous generation seeketh after a sign*. This is found in the New Testament book of Matthew 16:4, first part. Herod had killed John the Baptist because John told him he had committed adultery in marrying his own brother's wife (while his brother was still alive). Herod later thought Jesus was John come back to life to cause problems for him in Judea because he had been responsible for John's death. (He thought this was a 'sign'.) Israel had been told not to look to "seers" and other "diviners of signs", but to their God only for answers. Old Testament book of Deuteronomy 18: 9-15. God did not say those others did not have ability to do certain things, only that Israel was not to do things that way themselves. They were being given a new way to live that would transcend the way the nations around them lived.

OVERLAPPING POINTS

This point of teaching with the Bible overlaps with other points even as the *Law* is all bound up together. We can shine a light on a certain part of it for a moment and learn from it, but it all must be taken together.

Jesus told his disciples where to cast their nets in order to get across to them that *He* would provide the increase. He was going to make them fishers of men and would provide the abundant catch with men even as with the fish *if they would heed and cast their nets where he directed them.*

We find that God is no respecter of persons, New Testament book of Acts 10: 34 *Then Peter opened his mouth, and said, Of a truth I perceive that God is no respecter of persons:* This being so, it behooves all of us to inquire of God where to cast our nets in any situation, be it home; work; play; socializing; family; health; wealth...in fact, in any area and about anything at all. This will require us being a lot more diligent than we have been in our lives, moment to moment. We will need to examine ourselves, our thoughts, feelings, and actions, in order to determine whether we are casting our nets in the right direction, because God says in the New Testament book of Matthew 17: 16-20 (paraphrased) *By their fruit you shall know them.* Fruit is what we produce by our thoughts, words, and actions, whether we consider it important or mundane at the time.

God grant us to produce good fruit and to cast our nets in the right direction that we may have the abundant life and catch Jesus said he came for and that we may honor God in every part of our lives.

SELF-ESTEEM

In this article I will talk about *self-esteem*, and one of the ideas or concepts we use that we don't realize not only limits us but shows our lack of self-esteem.

In particular, the one where we feel or say, "You can't be anybody because I know you." *You* can't be anybody because *I know you*! That simply speaks for itself.

Jesus was subject to this same bias. In the New Testament of the Bible he said, *A prophet is not without honor, save in his own country, and in his own house.* Matthew 13:57. We read in Matthew 13:54-56 *And when he was come into his own country, he taught them in the synagogue, insomuch that they were astonished, and said, Whence hath this man this wisdom, and these mighty works? (55) Is not this the carpenter's son? Is not his mother called Mary? And his brethren, James, and Joses, and Simon, and Judas? (56) and his sisters, are they not all with us? Whence then hath this man all these things?* Verse 57 goes on to say, *And they were offended in him.* (Because *they knew him.*) In other words, how could he have this special ability when all the rest were "normal"— (like them).

I tend to think we live our lives in ignorance more so than in knowledge. The people had ability. They had knowledge. They even had great teachers. But they, as we all have the tendency to do, liked everything neatly boxed up and labeled so they could feel they were in control by virtue of putting things in their own little niche and not having to really think about them. Just automatic response. We live our lives on autopilot, it seems.

I don't know where this, seemingly innate, lack of self-esteem comes from unless it stems from the Garden of Eden story and our first parents found in The Old Testament book of Genesis 2: 16-17 *And the Lord God commanded the man, saying, of every tree of the garden thou mayest freely eat: But of the tree of the knowledge of good and evil, thou shalt not eat of it: for in the day that thou eatest thereof thou shalt surely die.*

My personal belief is that everything serves a purpose. This is how I view events mentioned in the Bible. They are there for us to learn from, and, as such, the lessons run much deeper than we think. For instance: The serpent in Genesis that spoke to Eve. In the account of the *tree of knowledge of good and evil*, found in the Old Testament book of Genesis 3: 1-5, the serpent implied that God was withholding something from them. Something desirable to make them wise (like God), and that He, God, didn't think that they were good enough to have this knowledge so he told them if they ate of it, they would surely die (to scare them away from partaking of it?).

At this point I don't know if they even understood what it would mean to *die*, unless they'd had the experience of witnessing death in the Garden of some of the other creatures that lived there. However, there is no indication of this mentioned in the Bible.

But the serpent told them they would <u>not</u> surely die as God had said, and that God knew better, just as he, the serpent did, but that they were not intelligent enough to grasp this is implied. So here was a creature in the Garden who had knowledge God had that was being withheld from them, who were also creations of God. Why? What was wrong with them? Why did God not want them to have the knowledge since this 'lowly' beast had it already? The Bible says Genesis 3:1 *Now the serpent was more* subtil *than any beast of the field which the Lord God had made.* It is also indicated that it went upright before God's curse was pronounced upon it. Genesis 3:14 And *the Lord God said unto the serpent, Because thou hast done this, thou art cursed above all cattle, and above every beast of the field, upon thy belly shalt thou go, and dust shalt thou eat all the days of thy life:*

It is interesting to note that this creature *talked* to Eve. Did *all* the creatures have this ability and just this one saw fit to "ruffle the waters", so to speak, by telling them what it did? And why just to this *human* creation? Possibly because they were the only ones told <u>not</u> to eat of that tree. How did this creature know what God had told them? I think it most likely that *all* the creatures knew what God had told them though they didn't talk to the humans about it.

Then, along came this serpent, who seemed to take issue with these who were created in the image and likeness of God, after the God kind, and were given dominion and rulership over all the earth and all the beasts of the earth (including the serpents). Shouldn't they at least, be able to eat of the tree without dying. After all, they were created after the God kind and God doesn't die. Shouldn't they have this knowledge and ability too?

THE CONSEQUENCES

Following the above account, we know that they *did* eat of the tree with what has always been thought of as disastrous results—a good indication they did not fear dying or even know what it meant. Mankind has since feared dying, disappearing as it were, forever, and blaming this problem on their progenitors Adam and Eve.

Once they were cast out from the Garden of Eden, or the Paradise of God as it is sometimes referred to, and had to 'scratch out' a living, the possibility of them developing a lack of self-esteem was great. They'd had it all and lost it all, or so they thought. People today that lose their wealth tend to feel a loss of self-esteem, as if their wealth gave them their worth.

Now God did not leave them comfortless. He gave them a promise of a son to come who would deliver them from their dilemma. We all tend to think these promises will take place in our time, and Eve was no different, for upon the birth of her son Cain she said, *I have gotten a man from the Lord.* Old Testament book of Genesis 4: 1. In the KJV there is the number '1' by the name Cain, and in the middle margin it is rendered *Acquired*, meaning she thought she had gotten the promised son. But when Cain killed his brother Abel (same chapter), they knew he could not be the son of promise which would only add to their lack of self-esteem. They still were not good enough to receive the one God had promised and were therefore still being punished by God by withholding it from them, (they thought).

We know today that it would be many generations before the *Promised One* would come on the scene. A lack of understanding of this would lead people to believe they are still lacking in something that keeps them from receiving and restoring their self-esteem. And if they are lacking, so is everyone else! Therefore, no one else could be anything because *we* know *we* aren't, and they can't be because we know they can't be any better than us.

FALSE HUMILITY—SAME AS PRIDE

In the New Testament book of Colossians 2: 18 we are warned of *voluntary (false) humility and being vainly puffed up by the fleshly mind*. Because one can become *proud* of his *humble* state and in doing so is no better than those who take pride in their wealthy estate. We are told in the Old Testament book of Proverbs 16: 18 *Pride goeth before destruction and an haughty spirit before a fall*. There are examples of those who became prideful and haughty who were humbled by God. One of them is found in the Old Testament book of Daniel 4: Where Daniel interprets the king's dream which came to pass as he had been warned of. 29-37 *At the end of twelve months he walked in the palace of the kingdom of Babylon. (30) The king spake, and said, Is not this great Babylon, that I have built for the house of the kingdom by the might of my power, and for the honour of my majesty? (31) While the word was in the king's mouth, there fell a voice from heaven, saying, O king Neb-u-chad-nez-zar, to thee it is spoken; the kingdom is departed from thee. (32) And they shall drive thee from men, and thy dwelling shall be with the beasts of the field: they shall make thee to eat grass as oxen, and seven times shall pass over thee, until thou know the most High ruleth in the kingdom of men, and giveth it to whomsoever he will. (33) The same hour was the thing fulfilled upon Neb-u-chad-nez-zar: and he was driven from men, and did eat grass as oxen, and his body was wet with the dew of heaven, till his hairs were grown as eagles' feathers, and his nails like birds' claws. (34) At the end of the days I Neb-u-chad-nez-zar lifted up mine eyes unto heaven, and mine understanding returned unto me, and I blessed the most High, and I praised and honoured him that liveth forever, whose dominion is an everlasting dominion, and his kingdom is from generation to generation: (35) And all the inhabitants of the earth are reputed as nothing: and he doeth according to his will in the army of heaven, and among the inhabitants of the earth: and none can stay his hand, or say unto him, What doest thou? (36) At the same time my reason returned unto me; and for the glory of my kingdom, mine honour and brightness returned unto me; and my counsellors and my lords sought unto me; and I was established in my kingdom, and excellent majesty was added unto me. (37) Now I Neb-u-chad-nez-zar praise and extol and honour the King of heaven, all whose works are truth, and his ways judgment: and those that walk in pride he is able to abase.*

TRUE SELF-ESTEEM

We read in the New Testament book of Romans 12: 3 *For I say, through the grace given unto me, to every man that is among you, not to think of himself more highly than he ought to: but to think soberly, according as God hath dealt to every man the measure of faith.*

This attitude that some are better than others was prevalent even in the churches. The Jews considered the Gentiles unclean, but now they were part of the churches. As Paul goes on to show in verse 5, *For we, being many, are one body in Christ, and every one members one of another.*

If we are all One, there can be no part better than another for one cannot be divided or it is no longer one.

We are children and offspring of God. There can be no greater reason for self-esteem. But it is not something to be *proud* of, rather to be truly humbled by the wonder of it all. That God, who is no respecter of persons, New Testament book of Acts 10: 34, is our Father the same as Jesus', and our God, the same as Jesus'. New Testament book of John 20: 17 *Touch me not; for I am not yet ascended to my Father: but go to my brethren, and say unto them, I ascend unto my Father, and your Father, and to my God, and your God.*

It's time to stop looking down on ourselves and our brothers and sisters as being *nothing* because *we know them*, when in fact, we are *all* somebody as *Children and offspring of God.* Be thankful and appreciate one another and fulfill the Royal Law of Love, New Testament book of James 2: 8-9.

About the Author

Writing under the pen name G. S. Fernandez, Gayle Sealey Fernandez is a retired senior citizen who has had an interest in the Bible since childhood.

Originally writing poems and making up projects for the children in the church she attended, such as crossword puzzles, word search, scrambled words and stories based on the Bible—she moved into writing what would later become her articles.

Writing from her own experiences over the many years as a member of a Christian church, as well as the experiences of others who followed Christian doctrine; she perceived a need to explore more deeply the ideals and principles of the Bible—especially those of the New Testament teachings of Jesus. This led to the book *Beyond the Torn Veil* in which some of these ideals and principles are taken a step further than previously understood.

Ms. Fernandez lives in Luling, Louisiana in Saint Charles Parish.

Printed in the United States
by Baker & Taylor Publisher Services